Thank You ... ... my words. I hope you

America Matters:

Why We Should Care!

enjoy them.

James D Buthman

Cover photos by James D. Buthman
Author photo by James Morrison

Printed in the United States of America.

PoliticsandNature.com.
2008

America Matters:

Why We Should Care!

James Douglas Buthman

For Bill Hervey

Acknowledgements

There are many people who have been instrumental throughout the process of thinking and writing this book. My girlfriend, Jean Palumbo, was instrumental in putting this together. We discussed issues and ideas about everything over the past six years and she is a fantastic, lovely woman with a keen intellect and kind nature. She helped greatly with the process of editing, making sure some of my ideas were clear and understandable. My parents, Al and Nancy, my sister, Lisa Hanson, and my friend Tessa Milosevich all spent the time to read early versions of the manuscript and provided insight and encouragement in the process of pulling it all together. My brother Jay made a gallant effort to check out the conclusion at the last moment. James Morrison hiked with me to take the cover photos.

I could do little without my family and I would like to acknowledge my nieces and nephews who have or are coming of age and who should be involved in national debates. They are: Jessica, Geri, Cody, Christy, Nick, Sarah, Sam, Molly, Keila, Alyssa, Reece, Jake, and Mason Buthman, and Megan and Dylan Hanson. The future is bright for all of you. My nephew and niece Luke and Karla returned to God's arms in 1988 and never leave our thoughts, as I am sure they are looking down and helping all of us get through our earthly trials. There is also Jessica's daughter Olivia, born in 2007, for whom our decisions will make all the difference.

The rest of my brothers and in-laws, Dave and Leen, Dan and Wendy, Mark and Tammy, John, Jay's wife Robin, and Lisa's husband Eric also provided encouragement and lively discussions over the years. It's amazing how much can be accomplished with a little respect for alternative views and the love of family.

My grandparents, Ruth Smith and John Childe, and Elmer and Berniece Bostock, always taught hard work, respect for others, thoughtfulness, and kindness as well as a love of nature which has all gone into this book. My grandmothers both passed away in 2007, while I worked on bringing my thoughts together. They lived long and fruitful lives and I am blessed to have been close with them. My grandparents lived with love and honor, something we could all learn.

Bill Hervey, to whom the book is dedicated, was my mentor at Colorado State University. He was a passionate professor with boundless energy and knowledge. He is no longer with us but I know his enthusiasm for the relationship between people, which he knew was acted out on the political stage, lives on not only in his children but in the many students, like myself, he influenced over the years. He lived for ideas, practical ideas which guided human reality. He was a man with a vision who spoke with a magnificent intensity. He was well versed in the philosophy of Socrates and Plato, Aristotle, Aquinas, and Machiavelli. He was just as comfortable and he felt right at home discussing Jefferson, Madison, Hamilton, Frederick Douglass, and the great legal minds of American history. Bill Hervey was the best teacher I have ever had.

I would also like to acknowledge two other guiding forces who I was lucky enough to meet and work for during my graduate work at Northern Arizona University. Dr. Hanna Cortner and Dr. Jacqueline Vaughn, I cherish their wisdom and appreciate their knowledge about political realities. To list their positive qualities and the impact they had on my life and thinking would require a book of its own.

There are many people we know in life whose impact goes beyond what they would ever quite realize. These people help shape our destinies and mold our minds. Among those in my life: Brian Carper, Joan Miller, Ellen and Chad Roberts, Travis Vandermale, Tom Foreman, Scott Dietz, Don Scheid, Dave Doarn, Chris Hartman, Carol Thompson, Jeff Bishop, Todd Radunsky, Matt Hammond, Martin Collins, Daniel Josyetewa, Jim Hall, Bill Coverdale, Wes Flynn, Jesse Hatcher, Jordan Levy, Don March, Steve Kirsch, Steve (Bud) Palm, and Bob. There's also my dogs, Spike, Zoe, and Marley. And to Diane Rheim, who shows us how to conduct dialogue on her NPR radio program every day. And many others who probably deserve mention among people I met along the way. Thanks to all.

Contents

Introduction

It has been frequently remarked that it seems to have been reserved to the people of this country, by their conduct and example, to decide the important question, whether societies of men are really capable or not of establishing good government from reflection and choice, or whether they are forever destined to depend for their political constitutions on accident and force.[1]

~Alexander Hamilton: Federalist #1, 1788

During the turbulent times of our nation's birth, Hamilton wrote these words to motivate a skeptical public to ratify the newly-drafted Constitution. As Americans, we continually decide whether we can obtain good government or if the destiny of nations is determined only by wealth, influence, and fraud. It is as true in our own day as it was when the nation was formed. This book tries to convey the substance of American politics, which is too often argumentative, imbued with caustic commentary, and guided by visceral reactions. While it is true that two distinct parties offer different visions of what our country should be, and it is vital to know which side you are on, we don't need to engage in grave, battle-scarred rhetoric all of the time. Instead, we have to learn how to engage in constructive dialogue without resorting to resentment and fury.

"One nation under God" doesn't mean unquestioning allegiance to a single group, party, or ideology. The strength of our country lies in the diversity of opinion and thought of all citizens. Differences and disagreements are essential to a democracy. However, as participants, we must learn to discuss issues without impugning the loyalty, patriotism, or sanity of every philosophical adversary. In order to do this, we must educate ourselves about the issues and respect the rights of others to hold alternative views. If we do this, we will see that the challenges facing us are just that…challenges to be overcome.

It seems, at times, that the American public is more interested in the outcome of sporting competitions than of national and certainly local elections. The media, which panders to the public's appetites, presents more pre-game analysis regarding the skills and match-ups of two sports teams prior to a playoff game than it does regarding the qualifications and abilities of candidates during an election cycle. News coverage focuses on polling data to discover only which candidate is currently in the lead. However, polls and the pundit's analyses of them say little about why elections and governance should concern all Americans.

Perhaps this is why, for many, politics is just a game in which nobody wins except the officials who get elected, and maybe those who get paid to screech at each other on television. The media fails to examine in any detail the important issues like the underlying purpose and implications of legislation. Instead, it focuses on what sells—the name-calling and shady tricks that have been around since the beginning of politics. Negative campaigning is not new. Despite the assertions that the people—the electorate—do not like negative campaigning, it is effective, and can enhance a candidate's chances of winning. One thing is sure—negative campaigning is not going away. But the stakes are high. As citizens, we can influence which road our country takes into the future. We cannot afford to be led astray by negative campaign ads and misinformation.

I don't mean to say that all politics is dirty or that all politicians are greedy and corrupt individuals who play the game with their hands out, waiting to score the big money. Corruption certainly exists in D.C. and in the capitals across the nation, just like it does in the corporate world. But this is not the whole story.

Our democracy protects us against corruption in government—it provides checks and balances. If it did not, the United States would be no different than the Soviet Union of old or Communist China under Mao—no better than Castro's Cuba where the old man had for so long divvied up the wealth of his island among the few that the people forgot what choice and freedom were. It is even rumored that Russia's autocrat, Vladimir Putin, holds warm thoughts for the "joys" of the Soviet regime when the Kremlin could crush a man's hands for writing subversive materials and then lock him away for ten years in a Gulag, surrounded by the frozen Siberian tundra. Our form of government is complex, intricate, and difficult. This is democracy!

While political prisoners exist in this country, and justice has not always prevailed, we, the people of this nation, have the power to do something to right the wrongs and abuses of power. The United States can only become stronger when we stand with the little guy; when we look at the past honestly and learn from our mistakes; and when we laugh a bit at ourselves. We will continue to make it our time as long as we gather together and talk as concerned citizens about things like the budget deficit, social justice, and freedom. We need to grow in new ways, reconsider basic assumptions, focus on what we all agree are important issues and discuss them as people who care about our form of government, for it holds within it the promise of the future.

Whether the current re-birth of the social order comes out of a reformed Republican Party, a dynamic and diverse Democratic constituency, some upcoming independent organization, or a combination of all the above, we all need to re-think our relationship with politics. Americans can shape their destiny...this is exciting!

Presidential elections inspire and motivate people. They encourage civic participation that combines ideology with practical considerations about leadership, citizenship, and ideas. On November 5, 2008 we could witness a great awakening, where people become and stay engaged in uncovering the pieces to our nation's greatest puzzles. Or, we can retreat back into the shadows and continue to allow the rulers to administer their divisive policies. It is essential for regular people, Americans, to seek the sunlight and stay informed and involved after the election. We must watch those who we elect to public office. After all, they just hold the reins of command that we give to them in trust.

A republic, such as ours, is a representative government and it works because voters send delegates to conduct the tedious, dry jobs of legislating, budgeting, and oversight. Public policy is not exciting, thrilling, fashionable, or emotionally moving, but it is essential because it is the basic function of government. In return for their service, officials may be re-elected as long as they do their jobs well. When they fail, they return to civilian life, either voluntarily, when they get caught doing wrong, or by the will of the people expressed at the ballot.

Leaders have long been sent home for bad behavior or poor performance. John Adams, the second president, was even cut off at the knees in the election of 1800, when he lost his bid for a second term as the nation's chief executive. He was a great man and an original patriot but this nation is larger than any one man. Adams weathered many storms and would be familiar with the rough politics of our own day.

As the media knows, controversy sells. Dire warnings predict the downfall of America and shine a spotlight on every battle over dogma. Opposing sides, immovable, bicker over spurious arguments: business dies at the hands of environmental protection or industry destroys nature; the feds crush civil rights or civil rights wipe out family values; marijuana leads our youth down a path of destruction or marijuana laws are unconscionable; illegal immigration takes away jobs from Americans or without illegal immigrants no one will mow our lawns, pick our lettuce, or watch our children. Every affair descends into this sort of dichotomous and bitter conflagration. It is as if someone were to suggest: "you're either with us or against us?"[2]

I'm not calling for some sort of sweet, gentle, bi-partisan deliberation, devoid of passion, excitement, and enthusiasm. On the other hand, every debate need not follow the prescription created by the old "debate" show *Crossfire*, or that of current television and radio talk show formats which foment rage and frustration instead of examining our alternatives and suggesting constructive options which open and expand dialogue.

Just imagine what would be possible for the future of our nation if Americans realized how much America truly does matter; if we got more involved, took control of our destiny, and directed elected men and women to work for the public welfare.

So, here it is, an unabashed, unashamed defense of the system, those who live under its roof, and those working diligently to make it a better, safer, more moral place for us to thrive and live out our dreams.

Chapter One: How Did We Get Here?

Optimism and Negativity

We the People of the United States of America, in order to form a more perfect union, establish justice, insure domestic tranquility, provide for the common defence, promote the general Welfare, and secure the Blessings of Liberty to ourselves and our Posterity, do ordain and establish this Constitution for the United States of America.

~U.S. Constitution: Preamble[1]

What happened to the American dream? Modern revolutionaries scream out for change, transition, movement! It is as if townsfolk grab pitchforks, raise torches, let loose the dogs, and the mob is growing anxious while the monster spreads blight over the land, crushing spirits and scarring souls. The fiend takes different forms, upsetting the apple carts, stealing the produce, and trampling the commoners. It is time for the trumpet to sound calling the cavalry, rousing passion and raising expectations. The American dream is not dead but sleeping, awaiting the arrival of courage, honesty, and clarity.

Ideological battles don't die, they are transformational. Assuming that the Constitution endures through the next two hundred years, and there's no reason it shouldn't, tomorrow's society will be embroiled in new battles. Pundits will claim to know what is wrong and politicians will declare they will fix every problem. Candidates will argue that he or she will walk into their new office and renovate the building. However, the structure of the government precludes radical tendencies. The Constitution is, after all, a conservative document.

Daily news reports constantly bemoan the tremendously troubled times we live in. Perhaps this is true, but the country has survived much worse. A small band of wealthy landowners chose to start a rebellion in 1776, committing all they had—"lives...fortunes...and sacred honor"[2]—to a dream of independence. In 1814, British troops burned the recently constructed home of the president in the newly formed

1

capital. Slavery was abolished after one of our nation's bloodiest wars, waged from 1861 to 1865. In 1916 the country's young men traveled to Europe to bring an end to an insanity which gripped the world. The stock market crashed in 1929, leaving millions hopeless and penniless. For the second time, Franklin Roosevelt led the nation to war in Europe in 1942, leaving the women at home to work, once again saving our relatives on distant shores. We have grown and learned through it all.

After the Second World War, the black man decided he'd had enough of segregation, inequality, and racism. And in 1955, the Supreme Court of the land agreed with him, picking up again the long dark struggle for the soul of the United States. An entire decade was embroiled in madness as civil rights and the meaning of liberty were shaken to the core, ending in 1974 as a disgraced world leader waved to the people on the White House lawn and stepped onto the executive helicopter for the last time. Each epoch brings is own dangers and the current one is no different. The founders offered us the freedom to pursue liberty. There are no guarantees.

Today's challenges appear tame in comparison to some of those in the past. Sometimes, the arguments are downright astonishing in their lack of rationality: shopping is more important than freedom; the wealthy confront greater injustice than the poor and middle class; environmental protection is radical; voting and civic participation does not matter; and all government is evil. These arguments fail to get us anywhere.

Like it or not, our federal government enabled President Jefferson to purchase the Louisiana Territory, abolished slavery, gave workers the right to organize, helped women earn the vote, and finally killed off Jim Crowe. We still have a great deal of work to do, but the current issues don't have the stark qualities we saw in the past. This leads to a polarized, muddled, and confused democracy, in which officials appeal to only their base and warn of the evils of any opposition. Too often, we allow them to succeed in the politics of negativity.

During each election cycle, experts warn about citizen carelessness. The professionals who study such things gasp at low political participation. Invariably, people cite disgust with both major parties, and politics in general, as reasons for taking no part in what we perceive to be a game with no winners, save special interest groups and corrupt politicians. People think politicians never get anything done because they don't really work, so why take part in the charade?

People gather around the proverbial water cooler and chat about such things as investments, TV shows, Hollywood gossip, and football. Many think there is nothing they can do about the current government or the fate of the nation, so they tune out the political debate. Whoever first said "you can't fight city hall" created false hopelessness based on the assumption that America does not, in fact, matter.

If you really want something done, storm into city hall, run for office, write letters, support non-profit groups, attend public meetings, protest, wave signs, hang a flag, start a blog, burn your money in front of Wall Street, join groups, give to political campaigns, work up the corporate ladder into a position of authority, volunteer, read, think, boycott products fashioned on injustice or environmental destruction, speak out, listen to others, learn about your government, take action. What is democracy if not the people's ability to shake up city hall?

Political battles are amusing and intriguing, but also essential for the path of liberty. Casualties have piled up in the pursuit of justice and freedom in this country. As Americans we enjoy the benefits of over two hundred years of contributions from dedicated individuals who generated a wealth of knowledge. The United States endured war, depression, and racism. We are stronger for our collective evolution, something all citizens can, and ought to, take pride in.

We should learn to appreciate the country we call home, study how we can make a difference, and never underestimate the possibilities. Each of us can encourage dialogue and strive to teach each other how to respect our differences, while holding fast to justice. This is how we build a prosperous nation with an unwavering commitment to fairness and integrity. The country's original documents—the Declaration of Independence, the Constitution, the Bill of Rights—form a covenant between the founding fathers, and past, present, and future generations.

The Constitution provides the structure for a stable government. However, it is not a staid and stagnant document awaiting strict constructionist interpretation of original intent. It does not offer the solution to every problem we are likely to face but it gives us the flexibility to adapt to changing circumstances. The founders could not have foreseen all the issues that would confront future generations, and we cannot know exactly how they would have addressed such things as civil rights, education, medical care, or environmental degradation. The Constitution is a living, breathing contract that offers us the rare chance to adapt our government to meet our needs and address the requirements of a changing society. Too often, though, instead of using this document as a roadmap, we get sidetracked by stale, outdated arguments that seek to place blame and divert our attention from the important work we should be doing.

If we, the people of this great nation, do not avail ourselves of the protections and privileges provided by the Constitution; if we fail to question our government and investigate its actions, then we run the risk of losing control of a runaway train. The Bush administration took advantage of the people's fear and acquiescence after September 11, 2001 and pursued an agenda supported by awesome executive privilege. Their reasoning went something like this: The U.S. is the most powerful nation in the world; the president is the chief executive of the nation and nothing, not even Congress or the people, should constrain the authority of the president. According to the Bush administration, truth was whatever they said it was.

This ideological twisting backfired on them in the end, but along the way, few dared question them—not the press, not Congress, and very few of the people. The Administration was allowed to run rampant like that old familiar bull in the china shop, trampling individual rights, disregarding fiscal responsibility, ruthlessly attacking political enemies, decimating environmental protections, and changing justifications regularly to support military intervention in Iraq. We gave them carte blanche to manage our affairs. This is never good, no matter what faction holds the public trust. Whenever one party gathers too much influence, it often falls short in the areas of integrity, honesty, and reliability.

Citizens need to take back the government from the short-sighted greedheads who run the show by reminding officials that they work for us and constantly admonishing them to keep the faith of office. This is unlikely to happen unless we take a more active role—seek out the facts, communicate with our representatives, and "hire" people with the will to govern effectively and conscientiously, instead of ideological purists, who chase their own agenda, demonize the opposition, and refuse to compromise. We can create a better future for our country, but we must acknowledge the lessons of the past, talk more, listen more, learn more, and participate. People must reject the simplistic arguments of us versus them. Modern issues are complex and all sides of an argument have some merit. We must craft solutions that take into consideration different points of view.

The government is just a reflection of us. If the public is not willing to discuss issues openly and question actions, our representatives won't talk about them either. The result can be graft and neglect and we should not be surprised when things go terribly wrong: the deficit is enormous, the response to Katrina was a disaster, the conduct of foreign policy has been short sighted and damaging to our international prestige, and the public is disenchanted. The bi-partisan bills of the past seven years, No-Child Left Behind and Medicare Prescription Drug Coverage, were unmitigated disasters with little popular support or understanding. Overall, federal management just seems to be a sham. Still, as pragmatic and conscientious people, if we choose, Americans can move mountains and reign in the crippling consolidation of power by either of the largest political parties.

Pragmatic America

I think that in no country in the civilized world is less attention paid to philosophy than in the United States. The Americans have no philosophical school of their own; and they care but little for all the schools into which Europe is divided, the very names of which are scarcely known to them...without ever having taken the trouble to define the rules of a philosophical method, they are in possession of one, common to the whole people.

~Alexis de Tocqueville, 1835[3]

Europeans poke fun at American pragmatism. They concern themselves with lofty, metaphysical musings of the state of being and things of this nature. However, these highly elevated philosophical ponderings don't interest Americans, who tend to see problems and try to solve them. Philosophers such as Sartre, Hegel, and Kant do not excite the American imagination. Our philosophy developed out of the regimens of farm life and the entrepreneurial spirit that emerged from the cities. In America, people had things to do and little time for idle ponderings. Like Voltaire's hero, Candide, we decided long ago it was best to cultivate our own gardens, not to continually worry over odd theories probing for the meaning of it all. In the beginning, there was the Good Book—what else could anyone possibly need?

In truth, we haven't been pragmatic in the way we govern ourselves lately. This country has grown from a loose confederation of independent states into a centralized conglomeration wherein states, municipalities, and individuals now find themselves obliged to conform to the dictates of the center of power in Washington, D.C.

A political theory dear to the Republican Party advocates the destruction of the federal government because it is too large, too powerful, too divisive, and too far removed from the wants and needs of real people in the heartland. This is a powerful idea. However, while Americans prefer an uncomplicated life, we find ourselves leading a complex global society. Not only is eliminating the federal government unrealistic, this approach has been only selectively pursued to advance personal agendas. The reach of government has not been reduced, and we usually neglect to question why.

The federal government spends over three trillion dollars per year.[4] According to the U.S. Department of Labor, the federal government alone employs 1.8 million people, excluding the U.S. Post Office, making it the nation's number one employer,[5] ahead of Wal-Mart (boasting 1.2 million employees).[6] For good or ill, our government affects all of us...every day. No matter how noble the ideal "that government is best which governs least,"[7] the federal reach will not shrink any time soon without realistic, practical policies which take into consideration the reasons for federal growth.

When people demand greater reliance on market forces, we need to have honest conversations about moral values and social responsibility. The free market provides incentives for growth, job creation, the pursuit of profit, and technological advances. It does not deal well with poverty, education, public lands, pollution, crime prevention, disaster relief, environmental clean-up and, quite possibly, health care. A pragmatic nation needs to confront these issues constructively.

The concept of letting market forces prevail totally unfettered is flawed. Cutting regulations on banking—sounds great—until it leads to a tragedy for home owners and government has to bail our the banks. Laying off public workers and privatizing labor within federal agencies—sounds wonderful—until we consider that it actually costs more and hiring private companies instead of using public employees creates incentives for corruption. Furthermore, getting rid of taxes on businesses for cleaning up the country's most toxic dump sites is great for business, but not for the rest of society, when the funds are depleted and our land and water is still polluted.

In actuality, policies such as these pervert the free market and leave citizens holding the bag. We need to truly be pragmatic and carefully consider the choices we face from all sides, including all possible consequences of our actions. Then we can get a better handle on our challenges and have more fulfilling discussions about the future.

Negotiation vs. Confrontation

But what is government itself but the greatest of all reflections on human nature?

~James Madison: Federalist #51, 1788[8]

A confrontational tenor now directs the national discourse. People seem to think it essential to take sides and to do so with a vengeance. Civility is losing the battle to malicious rhetoric. This is evident when voters elect those who wage the most depressing campaigns. Negativity and confrontation have reached epic levels and voters are turned off because neither helps us elect the most qualified, hard working candidates. Regrettably, as more folks tune out, hope of escaping the quagmire we have constructed becomes more elusive.

It is important to realize that arguments and passionate debate are fundamental to democracy. The famous relationship between President Ronald Reagan and Speaker of the House Tip O'Neil illustrates how politicians with completely different world views can vigorously argue over policies and priorities, and remain friends while still getting the work of the state done. Reagan and O'Neil didn't appear to agree on much of anything and they debated heatedly. But throughout their partnership they maintained respect and admiration for one another. They were able to work together, compromise, and move the country forward.

An amazing amount of negotiation goes on within the halls of government and this is absolutely necessary for the preservation of a strong and stable democracy. Negotiation occurs at every level: within and between the Senate and the House of Representatives, between Congress and the President, between lobbyists and representatives, and among federal, state, and local governments. Everywhere in government you will find a lot of talking and a fair amount of accomplishments.

On the other hand, some say negotiation and compromise facilitate weakness and undercuts ideological purity. Tom Delay, a former Republican leader in the U.S. House of Representatives, was a big proponent of the "crush the opposition at all cost" method of political achievement. But voters saw the commitment to raw power at any cost and reacted against it, eventually voting Delay out of office. Tom lumbered back to Texas confronting a new villain in the form of a prosecutor. No matter which party gains the gavel, they would do well to realize small mindedness and petty machine politics don't work well anymore. Negotiation is a key to superior policy decisions—and this is likely to keep a party in power.

Often, when times get rough, as they are now, respect and admiration seem to get lost and bitter invective becomes pervasive. The economy is flagging, debt is ballooning, citizens are nervous or downright scared, the environment is threatened, and government officials now seem to focus on confrontation instead of negotiation. Times like ours endanger compromise as legislators vote along strict party lines, very often not in the best interest of the nation. It is when things seem dark and dreary that politicians have been known to act like children, unable to even be in the same room with one another. When this happens, the system begins to falter and it is at risk of breaking down.

All of us can take things a little lighter and learn from the lessons of the past. Liberals and conservatives both believe in the ability of a free and just society to meet social needs. There are underlying differences about how to move forward but serious negotiations can resolve these distinctions. They do every year.

The Role of Politics

If men were angels, no government would be necessary. If angels were to govern men, neither external nor internal controls on government would be necessary.[9]

~James Madison, Federalist #51, 1788

Politics is the means by which we decide what we want as a society, how we plan to achieve our goals, and the way we argue and discuss policy, theories, and practice. In essence, it is how social choices are made. Politics can be overwhelming. It can be dirty, unjust, wrong, and ineffective. Politics is also fascinating and it enriches our social fabric. For centuries it has been seen as the most noble of human endeavors. This is because all other pursuits live under the political umbrella.

The United States was founded upon and continues to be nurtured by free expression and the flow of ideas. People in this country enjoy the right to fight for their beliefs, hopes, and dreams. The Declaration of Independence states that the purpose of government is to safeguard the rights of "life, liberty, and the pursuit of happiness."[10] Furthermore the Creator provides these rights to all people. Our nation's founding documents codified an expansive concept of liberty which we have struggled to achieve ever since and this is a never ending process.

American political history is astonishing in the breadth of accomplishments and the depth of commitment to intellectual, economic, and spiritual growth. Our political system assures us the freedom to hold different beliefs and values, while binding us together. It allows free individuals to pursue their visions and to enjoy the fruits of their labor. It should also level the economic playing field, even though it may not always succeed.

Thomas Jefferson believed that if we allow liberty to stagnate, if we cease to strive for liberty, it will die. Advocating consistent reform, he argued that we should continually challenge the status quo with intelligence, thought, and deed in order to ensure that our government conforms to democratic principles. The elites should never gain too much power and the government should adapt to reflect current realities. All systems require revision, like upkeep on a house or maintenance of roads and bridges. Politics allows us, as individuals, to take part in our own preservation.

It is imperative that we don't lose sight of the meaning and the true power of the nation. The words upon which it was created inspired people to achieve great things and they continue to be relevant in our global age. Politics in America is unique because we can play a role in national discussions and we can provide guidance to a changing world.

The ideology dominating twenty-first century social discourse is grounded in the free market. But without politics, America will fall into the trap of being merely a nation committed to the struggle for power and economic dominance. Adam Smith, the father of capitalism, wrote *The Wealth of Nations* in 1776 in England while our founders wrote of separation from the tyranny of the king. Smith's ideas of a free market guided by an invisible hand has directed our thinking ever since. However, we must be aware that corporate dominance obstructs the free market and this leads us to disregard market failures—and market failures rear their ugly heads all the time.

Smith's analysis of capitalism contains critical insight but our political discussions have relied too heavily on his thoughts of economic freedom while we have neglected our own nation's commitment to personal freedom. Even Smith believed some government was required for stable economics and society. We need a more substantive politics which will really dissect our national, philosophical assumptions. This may enhance our dialogues because a deeper understanding of the present demands a fuller knowledge of the past. Moving forward blindly will only move us backwards. American history is long, complex, and multifaceted and we can not rely on simplistic slogans.

The federal government, at its worst is necessary, and, at its best, it does immeasurable good. This country achieved great things in the 20th century, including: creating interstate highways, the space program, The Tennessee Valley Authority, The Civil Rights Act of 1965, The Voting Rights Act of 1965, and The Civilian Conservation Corps. The last century saw the expansion of worker's rights, women's rights, the abolition of state sponsored segregation, an emphasis on education, and increased urgency over environmental protection. These are positive achievements and it is frustrating when they are dismissed as futile.

The federal government constructed the Forest Service, the National Park Service, the Federal Communications Commission, the Environmental Protection Agency, the Federal Aviation Administration and the Federal Emergency Management Agency. It took steps to expand personal freedom and security. Social Security, Medicare, and Medicaid evolved with changing retirement and healthcare needs. Politics was used to expand individual rights, raise awareness of nature, stabilize the business climate, create technological advances, and establish retirement security. It isn't a bad record.

There will never be another nation like The United States of America. Never has the world seen the freedom of opportunity and cohesiveness within such a diverse nation. This is why U.S. citizens are so proud of our country. But as Jefferson suggested, as we move into the new century, we must reform programs, restructure taxes, revitalize our educational infrastructure, and face hard questions over war and peace. In working towards these goals, politics, debate, and compromise will be at the heart of how we conduct our affairs or we will never get anywhere.

Corruption will not go away. It exists in every facet of life. People cheat, lie, and steal in business, in education, in law, and in science. They do so in government as well. At least in a republic, we have a chance of catching inept or dishonest politicians. Good government is dead only when we lose interest and give up on it. Only then can the rise of tyrants, thugs, and dumb brutes really begin.

Chapter Two: American Perils

Simplify, Demonize, and Control

There is a new meanness on both sides...and no more humor.[1]

~Hunter Thompson, 1969

The political process has often been boiled down to its most base aspects...simplify the argument and demonize the opposition in order to gain control of the system. Politics seems so mean and petty these days. Leaders on each side of the political aisle hunker down in the trenches and wait until their trained hyenas smell blood and then they pounce, attacking their opponents, not for the good of the nation, but for political posturing. As much as we would like for this to change—it will not happen any time soon. This is serious business with real stakes—possibly wealth, definitely power, and, for some, a place in the history books.

Each side continually jockeys for position. People perceive Congress as the ultimate arena—a cage match pitting two ignorant giants bashing each other for the prize of control over public resources. Bills are brought to the floor with so many agendas attached that voting against one provision may unwittingly place a legislator on the wrong side of another issue, providing their opponents with fresh campaign fodder. One is tempted to simply give up, cash in your chips, head home, call it a day, and avoid thinking about self government.

Of course, demonizing opponents is standard fare in American politics. Long ago, after George Washington rode away from the White House and into history, demonizing in party politics took its rightful place in the United States. John Adams and Thomas Jefferson wrote about their disdain for and concern over the negative effects that factions had on the young republic...but they engaged in the practice just the same.

Jefferson was more adept at using the new divisions created by Washington's departure, and Adams lost his bid for re-election. The election of 1800 showed how low partisan politics could go. Adams loyalists accused Jefferson of being a Francophile who would assuredly sell the country to the French, while Jeffersonians accused Adams of an unhealthy appetite for monarchy. Even before 1800, the first divisive election in our history, the popular press poked fun at George Washington. It seems no one has ever been safe.

Today, liberalism has become the object of spite. Even liberals wish to avoid being tarred and feathered with the term. Because our current understanding of liberalism is vague and inconsistent, it gives the anti-liberal bloc the room to define it as they like, encouraging the name-calling that derails the discussion over real agendas. This modern usage is more representative of dishonest manipulation than authentic differences. It can be used to divide and conquer because labels eliminate the need for constructive strategies. The word liberal is consciously disparaged along with Communism and Socialism. Liberals, for their part, have failed to craft a competing narrative explaining their philosophy, making it even tougher to fend off the attacks.

It has long been easy to convince voters of liberals' evil intentions. The claim is that they tax hard workers and businesses to enable exorbitant spending on the "nanny state".[2] William F. Buckley and Barry Goldwater began to weave this storyline into the U.S. mainstream beginning in the 1950s and 1960s. Lyndon Johnson routed Goldwater in the 1964 election but Goldwater had the last laugh. He planted the seeds of conservative thinking which has produced fruit for forty years. Today, even those who claim to be above the fray step in and take shots at liberals to make a point or get a cheap laugh.

Rush Limbaugh, a thriving mainstream media voice, who has successfully motivated Americans to think about politics for over fifteen years, offers assurances to his audience that he is above debasing forms of political discourse. Consider what is written on page 186 of his best selling 1992 book *The Way Things Ought to Be*:

> *Name-calling becomes a substitute for meaningful debate of the issues and it works quite well in the political arena. That is unfortunate, because the name-*

calling, while it may have a chilling effect on the genuine discussion of issues, does nothing to satisfy the millions of people who share the views of those who are the targets of those insults.[3]

You see, he claims to be an honest broker of information. He argues against, in his categorical fashion, the degrading nature of such activities grounded in name calling...then he launches into a tirade against his foes. Within three pages, on page 189, Mr. Limbaugh writes:

Many feminist leaders are humorless, militant, pugnacious, and very unhappy people who do not want to equalize the status of women, but instead want to irreversibly alienate women from men and vice versa.[4]

How quickly he forgot not to call names. A quick perusal of Limbaugh's best selling tome produces ample evidence illustrating how much faith he actually puts on name calling and demonization. In reality, he has helped raise these perverted forms of dialogue into an art form—and he's made a very decent living doing so.

On page xiii (that's in his "advisory section—the first page of the book beyond acknowledgements), Limbaugh pens:

So beware: there are people out there—Communists, Socialists, Environmentalist Wackos, Feminazis, Liberal Democrats, militant Vegetarians, Animal Rights Extremists, Liberal Elitists—who will try to prevent you from reading this book.[5]

On page 15, he explains how "a few angry liberals" are out to get him. On page 21, the reader learns liberals aren't funny, conservatives are: "most liberals are too busy mired in misery and handwringing and doing what they can to spread it around."[6] On page 27 he opines it is "the liberals, you see, [who] do not want to confront conservative ideas; they just attack conservatives as a group, and particularly their motives."[7]

Mr. Limbaugh's extremist rhetoric leaves no space for honest talk over creative opinions. In the book there is no attempt to bring people together to craft useful solutions to modern dilemmas. However, it should never be used to make him more than he seems to be...a somewhat sad, ill tempered man who likes to talk a lot. One thing is sure, it takes stamina to keep up the divisiveness every day. He's got that going for him.

The point here is to unveil the insane lengths someone with a tremendous following is willing to go to attack the enemy (his fellow citizens) and the outlandish generalizations used to justify the madness. To be sure, evidence can easily be dug up of groups attacking Republicans with the same venality and tastelessness but it is hard to argue with the success of conservative anger and it is highly doubtful any liberal blog or other source of mindless invective on the left reaches anywhere near the mass audience of the right wing.

The Republican Party engineered its own downfall through corruption and base neglect of the public trust, not by some liberal conspiracy. Still, angry conservatives rail against "liberals." This is interesting but not very productive.

By 1996, much of the public believed that the Republican Party and President Bush had used the offices entrusted to them as if they were a secret playground, providing a perfect example of what happens as public input declines and the rulers are left to feed at the public trough on pure ideology and unfettered control.

Democrats took over Congress in 2006. They capitalized on Republican self-implosion because voters judged that the ruling party was captured by zealots working to stifle open debate, actively destroying the foundations of democracy.

It is to be seen if the Democrats can move the country in a constructive direction but the government is theirs to lose. Unfortunately, they have not yet shown the ability to rise above the bickering and they have so far failed to inspire a disenchanted public. They had moved markedly to the political middle in 2006 and this helped them win Congress but they must exhibit exemplary conduct and uphold American values; transparency, accountability, leadership, fiscal responsibility, working with the minority, and respecting diversity, in order to re-capture the confidence of the people. They will lose the majority quickly if they fail to honor these principles. After all, both parties have their demons.

Spirited debate is at the core of political practice but national arguments need to be respectful. They do not need to be spiteful. Principles are important and passion is a key to freedom. Free expression is a core belief making the United States what it is and it needs to be protected at all costs. Heated arguments can expand the mind and invigorate the soul. But we can do this with an appreciation for one another's views while searching for areas where we can agree.

The Progressive Impact

Still other Republican leaders have insisted on calling themselves "progressive" Conservatives. These formulations are tantamount to an admission that Conservativism is a narrow, mechanistic economic theory that may work very well as a bookkeeper's guide, but cannot be relied upon as a comprehensive political philosophy.[8]

~Barry Goldwater, 1960

Barry Goldwater, an early proponent of the modern conservative movement, took on Republicans back in the 1960s for straying from their roots and calling themselves progressives. It appears Barry held a certain contempt for those who believed in this political terminology.

Progressives, in his opinion, sold out conservative values, like sheep lacking a shepherd, winding through the political morass without a compass and with no foundation for the entire being. They held on to a foolish and half baked idealism following the tenets of the day but lacking true courage and spirit. Barry advocated individual responsibility and small government in all cases except national defense. He was a man swimming against the tides in the 1960s.

Modern liberals have reached the same pinnacle deemed so unworthy by Goldwater. They seem to be gasping for air, failing to look to the past for success and giving in to the anti-government screed dominating our airwaves. They have lost the argument, given up the ghost, and gone a new way. Many have taken to calling themselves progressives. And so the pendulum swings.

Progressives do have a long and storied history in the United States but mostly as spoilers or unadulterated pragmatists seeking to combine the best elements of idealism with current trends to reform and rejuvenate America. Teddy Roosevelt became so heavily endowed with a belief in a better way that he left the Republicans after his two terms in the Oval Office, helped form the Progressive Party in 1912, and ran on its ticket. However, he merely helped to split the Republican vote thus yanking William Howard Taft from the White House and securing the presidency for Woodrow Wilson.

History does not bode well for the self-described progressive movement in America today. Progressivism is the effort on the part of middle of the road folks to steer around the dangerous and deadly turns of partisan politics. Back in the 1960s conservatives were considered out of the mainstream, heartless and cruel, willing to let the poor wallow in the mud and the grime and they lost the national debate for a long period of time. But Barry was undaunted. He even took Ike to task for differentiating social from fiscal conservativism.

The same thing is happening today with liberals. They turn away from a proud American tradition and call themselves progressives because they have lost their conviction. Most of us are middle of the road and we want a strong, free, and fair republic in which to pursue our aspirations.

This is why we shy from antagonistic labels and seek common ground. The way our government is constructed, officials have to work together and this is what we generally desire.

For this reason, progressive movements within the country have always held a broad appeal despite its losses. We want representatives who will stand by their convictions but who have the intelligence, forethought, and wisdom to work with others.

Reagan worked with a Democratic Congress and Clinton worked with Newt Gingrich's Republican Congress. We are not always going to all join hands together and we should not want this to happen. The contentious, close race of 2000 illustrates our divisions, the patriotic fervor following the events in 2001 proves our patriotism, and the slim margin voting for the President in 2004 demonstrates that not all Americans believe in one single authoritarian vision of the future.

Unfortunately, neither of the major political parties really captures the spirit of the people like they could. So much of this is because of the negativity and the quest for power between the two. It is ironic that one of the major protections against tyranny, this division of power, seems to reduce the ability of regular people to get involved in the political process and to make a real and lasting difference. This is where progressive candidates come into our world and prod the system into alternative directions. This is when grand scale citizen involvement with third parties makes change possible.

Liberty

Liberty the greatest of all earthly blessings—give us that precious jewel, and you may take every thing else...When the American spirit was in its youth, the language of America was different: Liberty, Sir, was then the primary object.[9]

~Patrick Henry, 1788

John Stuart Mill, author of *On Liberty*, a treatise of freedom, argued there was no justification for legislative intrusion into private lives unless the restricted action caused harm to others. In other words, there is no government right to enforce its desires on individuals for their own safety or to uphold social mores. This is the essence of social liberty but elected officials are too willing to restrict our choices in order to protect us from ourselves. This is no way to govern.

The United States, consumed by free market slogans, is losing reverence for individual autonomy. Liberty now means emancipation from business constraints as opposed to independence from corporate influence, customs, and militarism. This is a defining struggle in our century—difficult because it is not concrete, threats against it are not as clearly defined as they once were, and order dominates in the wake of

September, 2001. It is vital to remember that the defense of liberty is the essential aspiration of the United States.

So much talk of liberty today is dull. Corporate freedom is upheld as the progenitor of consumer rights and a vast portion of society just isn't interested. Liberty has become synonymous with license for the rich. Some argue it is important for Exxon-Mobil to be free of regulatory burdens while the general welfare suffers from our addiction to oil. Wal-Mart cries out at the inequity of restricting its growth while workers toiling in its stores struggle with low wages and often lack of health care.

Freedom! Shout prospectors clamoring to develop public lands thus denying the sources of spiritual renewal for millions of workers. Coal companies receive massive subsidies and are allowed to destroy the mountains of West Virginia. Multi-nationals are encouraged to outsource production and jobs. What ever happened to the liberty of the common man?

This relationship needs to be changed. The right to buy, consume, and develop is not the same as free thinking and unhindered action. A respect for liberty goes a long way to pointing the direction toward the future. Freedom strengthens the body and sharpens the mind. It opens doors, expands possibilities, and enhances our lives.

The ever present menace is the thirst for control. Fanatics consider those demanding answers as weak conspiracy theorists willfully betraying certain, narrow views our country. It is through this sense of super-patriotism that John Kerry and Max Cleland, decorated veterans, were attacked for being un-American.

It is disturbing when patriotism is called into question for political purposes. Arguing against the government is distinctly American. The First Amendment clearly states:

> *Congress shall make no law...abridging the freedom of speech, or of the press; or the right of the people peaceably to assemble, and to petition the government for a redress of grievances.*[10]

Powerful forces want to exert control over speech by demanding strict adherence to incensed views and they are willing to chastise any who exact honest answers from public officials. This harms our devotion to liberty.

Taking on liberty is akin to waging all out war on our traditions. The Bush Administration showed astonishingly little actual respect for liberty, despite its assurances to the contrary. As a result, John Kerry lost his bid for the presidency in 2004 by only three percent to a sitting president while the nation was at war...So much for the wonder of Karl Rove.

Rove has been hailed as a political genius for engineering two wins for President George W. Bush. In actuality, a true mastermind would have convinced his employer to broaden his coalition which would have led to a landslide victory in place of an astonishingly slim win. The threat to political liberty arises out of the desire of a small majority of the nation to squash alternative thinking and this is, and always has been, the real threat to liberty.

Active, thoughtful dissent is critical. The first move tyrants make is to crush anyone looking too closely at how things are managed. Free speech and expression are building blocks of the United States and they provide a voice to political minorities but in the modern context, we often rely on outdated economic conceptions and confuse corporate liberty with individual freedom.

Does freedom require us to turn our heads to corporate exploitation? Does freedom to develop open space outweigh the rights of citizens to keep wetlands as a natural buffer against hurricanes? Is the unhindered capacity to discover new oil and gas more important than the freedom to fish and hunt a healthy game population uncontaminated by toxic spills, roadways, traffic, and habitat destruction? How does a license to create tree farms impact the liberty to learn and grow from the serene beauty of hiking through the awesome expanse of an old growth forest? What is the trade off between the liberty of corporate coal manufacturers when balanced with the safety of its miners, affected communities downstream, or future generations who will never experience the wonder of certain West Virginia Mountains?

Is the freedom of the moneyed interests more important than the simple liberty of the commoner? Does selling off everything for short term gain make us more secure and successful? These questions lie at the center of the debate over modern freedom and we should talk about them honestly…with clarity and vision.

Anytime environmental protection or the rights of workers and citizens comes up against the bulwark of economics, dire warnings ring out over the horrid affects of regulation and taxation. These same voices are strangely silent about adverse consequences resulting from short sighted business practices.

America needs vibrant periods of renewal in order to grow and these only occur when committed and thoughtful citizens stand up to the mega-structures commanding from glass towers. We must never forget the importance of liberty and we always need to protect it from both government encroachment and corporate confusion.

The Founders

I conceive this new government to be one of those dangers...it will oppress and ruin the people.[11]

~Patrick Henry, 1988

Patrick Henry, revolutionary agitator, fiery orator, father of the rebellion, did not like the Constitution. Like so many men of the time, his views did not fit into a neat little box along with all the others. Every side of the political aisle claims the ancestry of the founding fathers. A conservative explains their views on the judiciary. Liberals speak of the Bill of Rights. Televangelists argue that God mattered most. Atheists point to Jefferson's private letters. Everyone needs to take a deep breath and think a bit more about the fights waged in Independence Hall. These men discussed everything and often disagreed with one another. Many were slave holding, wealthy, white males and none could foresee how the future would unfold.

After they emerged with a document setting out the framework for a new government, a public conversation emerged over ratification. This is why Alexander Hamilton, James Madison, and John Jay wrote the Federalist Papers; to convince citizens of the merits of the Constitution.

Conversely, plenty of revolutionaries regarded the Articles of Confederation; the initial, loose collection of states, as the ultimate form of union.

The Constitutional Convention was initially authorized only to revise the Articles, not abolish them. Tyranny was at the top of everyone's minds and it was all they could do to stomach the idea of a potent centralized system of control over states' rights. Many delegates and other men of reputation insisted on a series of restrictions on federal authority…a Bill of Rights.

The Bill of Rights was the ultimate check on authority mandating limits on government. It did this because the men debating the Constitution were well educated and they knew history. They understood the attack on liberty which is inevitable with unchecked power.

Today, it appears few of us think about the past unless we wish to illustrate knowledge of sports scores, statistics, and highlights. To truly restrain the boundaries of power, we need to concern ourselves with history, learn how we got here, ponder where we may go, and judge how reforms will affect popular programs.

The founding fathers belong to no ideology. Their diversity led to quarrels once they had escaped from the bonds of England. In reality, the human experience is not much different now. Human nature is the same as it has been for millennia. Petty jealousy, rage, desire, thirst for wealth and influence, all were present even in the time of Moses. The founders considered these things and crafted a system pitting the powerful against each other.

The checks and balances are intricate and widespread. Not only is authority diffused between the executive, legislative, and judicial branches, but it is defrayed by parties and between the federal, state, and local governments. The muscle of senators, the most influential members of each state, is diluted within the Senate. The size and extent of the republic even provides checks; distilling the passionate temper of the masses and reducing the capability a small body to enforce its will for a long period of time.

These are the wonders of the structure of our United States government. It is difficult for particular factions to control our entire social order. Instead of capturing the founders for narrow political purposes, we need to appreciate their diversity and strive to emulate their ability to strive for what is achievable.

Getting Beyond the Rhetoric

They say the world has become too complex for simple answers. They are wrong.[12]

~Ronald Reagan,

One way to get beyond rhetoric is to look for the humor. Conservative humor, as found in Limbaugh's book, can actually be funny in an odd, mean spirited sort of way, as can Liberal images of Dick Cheney as a monster, grumbling incoherently under his breath in anger while he is locked away in a basement to keep him from eating children. Get over it. If it makes a point...good—humor, at its best, does.

Each side has designs which can be expressed in bizarre ways. This too is part of the political process. Congress should never issue statements expressing outrage over any viewpoint...as they have done in recent years...even the most distasteful ones. The psychosis is mounting and it is hard to find the wit in the malicious rhetoric and back and forth predictions of ever-impending doom. The sky isn't actually falling, it is just turning gray.

Hubris (excessive pride) took down the Democrats in 1994. In 1992 they had it all and they flaunted it. Reagan was gone, Bush I had been ushered out of town, and Democrats controlled Congress and the White House. However, congressional leadership did not convey a positive message, infighting began, and they let it all slip out through their hands like a greased pig. They set themselves up for the fall and lost the debate over the future by ignoring the minority and governing as if they were the chosen ones. As a result, the Democratic Party spent twelve years in the political wilderness and they have not gotten out of the woods yet.

The Democrats must continue to readjust and moderate or else they'll be headed back to nature so fast it will make their heads spin. And if they become monolithic and careless then their future and the nation's is in great peril. Both parties need positive messages and honest messengers. Each side has pluses and minuses. Beneficial government is not overbearing but it is not callous either. We continually walk the tightrope between these two opposing philosophies.

Like the Democrats in 1993, Republicans also lost sight of the fact that they worked for the voters after they gained total control in 2001. They wanted it all—no messing around—they planned to set up shop in D.C. and hang out for a good long while. Once W entered 1600 Pennsylvania Avenue, the entire party structure decided it was no longer the people's house but they would re-fashion it into the house that George built.

These men and women convinced themselves they had beaten the Democrats so badly they would never get up. Republicans ran the show like a private circus, conferring favors back to the wealthy elite in the form of tax cuts and no-bid contracts, but they did not reduce spending. They only gutted the federal treasury and propped up a fantasy realm of seemingly sound fiscal order.

So, the self proclaimed party of fiscal discipline fell apart at the seams, gave it all away, sold out, lost focus, and just generally screwed up so bad the Democrats are getting back up. But they need to be careful. The federal government is important but Democrats have to understand that voters want limited government.

Many of us do want to reduce the size of the federal government, but we must beware or else calls for small government and responsibility will never be anything more than catchy slogans enriching special interests. We are always working to expand individual freedoms and the rights of citizens.

Jefferson wrote, in 1826:

May [the Declaration of Independence] be to the world, what I believe it will be (to some parts sooner, to others later, but finally to all), the signal of arousing men to burst the chains under which monkish ignorance and superstition had persuaded them to bind themselves, and to assume the blessings and security of self government. That form which we have substituted, restores the free right to the unbounded exercise of reason and freedom of opinion. All eyes are opened, or opening, to the rights of man. The general spread of the light of science has already laid open to every view the palpable truth, that the mass of mankind has not been born with saddles on their backs, nor a favored few booted and spurred, ready to ride them legitimately, by the grace of God. These are grounds of hope for others. For ourselves, let the annual return of this day forever refresh our recollections of these rights, and an undiminished devotion to them. [13]

In this letter, Jefferson laid out his vision of what the Declaration of Independence meant in his and for all time. His was a vision of civil rights and justice. Combat over the meaning of the past has turned acerbic and blinded Americans to our true heritage. Our complex, rich, and colorful history binds our generation to our forbearers and it provides concrete knowledge of what we can accomplish. The name-calling and shallow minded efforts to spin the multi-layered web of collective evolution into a single, simplistic, drab cocoon based on fatalism needs to be cast down into the pit of irrelevance.

We live at the dawn of the twenty first century! What an exciting time to be alive! We must all continue to rise against injustice and to take action when wrongs cross our paths. But we must do so with compassion, non-violence in our thoughts as well as in our acts and this requires respectful dialogue. It is urgent that we champion true liberty; it is the heart and soul of our nation and it is a longing placed within each human being by our Creator. It is the light which shines out among all nations from our shores. Weary travelers search for ways to reach these shores believing something better awaits them, like the wise men guided by the Star of Bethlehem, they chase freedom and opportunity.

Getting beyond the enraged rhetoric requires: a bit more understanding of political opposition; a smidgen of courtesy for others; a touch of consideration regarding their motives; a dash of comprehension about history and political theory; and a morsel of faith in our nation and in our ideals.

This doesn't mean don't fight the good fight. If you are a liberal, be a liberal. Don't take on the "progressive" label just because liberalism has been dragged through the mud. Dirt builds character. Conservatives are already very proud to be conservative. Stay proud. But give each other some respect. Thoughtful people disagree, sometimes passionately. This is how a free country operates.

Chapter Three: Manufacturing Crises

The End is Near

I am here concerned not so much by the abandonment of States' Rights by the national Democratic Party—an event that occurred some years ago when that party was captured by the Socialist ideologues in and about the labor movement—as by the unmistakable tendency of the Republican Party to adopt the same course. [1]

~Barry Goldwater, 1960

The end is always near in the United States. Pessimism grows out of every corner of the public square. Even those fighting against it are unable to hold it back. The mere position of demanding change argues the nation is heading down a forbidding road leading to an abyss of despair. The 2008 presidential contenders each vowed reform. Yet, there has been too much fear, too much talk of doom, and too little kindness.

People honestly believe Islamic terrorists hiding in the bulrushes around Washington D.C. are just waiting to take control of the White House. There are individuals who depend upon this fear. They Keep people from Wichita to Walla Walla up at night with nightmares of the imposition of Sharia law inevitably following the radicals' mushroom cloud. But fear quashes the thirst for liberty. Fear raises the specter of the final death toll for the American dream and it supports the fanaticism of the most prominently self-promoting super-patriots who don't have time for civility and independence. Once order overpowers freedom, the needs of the state will truly outweigh the rights of the individual.

At the same time, our country has been redefined based solely upon self interest. Reverence for the system is gone. Words written in history have become quaint relics of an irrelevant age. However, it is important that we remember there is not another government like it in history. It is too bad that some have simply become disengaged, believing certain thresholds of knowledge relate only to the influential few forming the top of the social pyramid.

Critical thinking belongs in everyone's realm. Political theory and practice work together. They are two sides of the same coin. But consistent voices bemoan blatant and ignorant uses of politics by elected officials and faceless bureaucrats. Intense factions grow out of the refusal to hear each other and then dialogue descends into a contest over who yells louder, in spite of validity. The inability to listen restricts the free flow of knowledge, impedes personal fulfillment, and creates an atmosphere of division permeating the public atmosphere.

The media often composes the symphony of despair breaking us down. Major stories appeal to the darkest recess of the human spirit. The long, tired march of depressing statistics makes their way in the seemingly endless repetition of the twenty four hour news cycle. The gossip erupts wholesale on so-called "analysis" programs aimed to convince the audience of the tragedy and horror of the latest Hollywood scandal and designed to illustrate how these reflect America.

News needs to be fast, original, imaginative, gripping, flat-out electrifying, and communicated in the few available moments between commercial breaks. It is mind-numbing. The same newscasts and redundant interviews fill time with the newest "breaking story". In depth discussions over policy aren't fun so television, radio, and internet outlets give up on them quickly. It is better if a story is bawdy, depraved, indecent, lecherous, reckless, salacious, and wild. Each time the chronicle is played, viewers are riveted to the television and engaged by whatever new information has been gathered since the previous hour.

Yes, we are constantly told the end is near. Any story meeting this qualification quickly reaches the top of the charts for the anchor, talk show host, or blogger. The greater the emotional pull of the story, the more time will be spent on it.

Everything is a crisis. The world is filled with people who are too thin, too fat, depressed, impotent, and scared. The newest drug is always available and it will solve all your problems—although it may create a few more. Lawsuits follow when it is discovered this or that drug caused this or that illness and, all the while, drug companies make billions of dollars, pay millions to their executive officers and the Man wants to lock folks up and throw away the key for growing or smoking or possessing marijuana.

It would all be too overwhelming and depressing without a sense of who we are as a nation and an understanding that, if we choose, we can alter our course and steer the ship of state away from its tragic course. The end is not near! We are just getting started! American ingenuity and drive can confront any difficulty. Hope has been the driving force in American politics for over 200 years and we have a long way to go but our democracy is vibrant and malleable. As long as we understand these facets of our nation, we have no fear of "the end."

Angry Amerika

To judge from the conduct of the opposite parties, we shall be led to conclude that they will mutually hope to evince the justness of their opinions, and to increase the number of their converts by the loudness of their declamations and by the bitterness of their invectives.[2]
~Alexander Hamilton, Federalist #1,1788

It is really quite astonishing how well the founding fathers understood human frailty. Listening to talk radio, one gets the feeling that no liberal believes in America. Tensions over questionable campaign tactics and outright attacks on loyalty are disturbing to those of us pondering over modern political discourse. Still, damaging ads have a long and storied tradition in our nation. However, it has become clear that anyone disagreeing with certain ideological stances is open to merciless harassment. The dominant view has become that we are all in this thing separately. Beware if you are foolish enough to buck this trend and to talk of a more noble vision of collective America. The sharks are swimming and they are ready to feed if you stray too far into the sea of ideas without conforming to their constricted view of humanity, economics, and country.

Ideology rules these days. This comes in waves within America. Back in 1800 the Alien and Sedition Acts passed to discourage immigration and create prison sentences for anyone speaking against the government. President Adams supported the laws. Outraged Jeffersonians initiated an all out assault against Adams and the newspapers printed vile attacks on the president. No, party politics and disparaging views based on ideological purity is nothing new. It is simply more widespread now through better communication mediums like radio, television, and the internet.

Yet it is important to remember political corruption occurs in all social orders. Those who know how to manage the crowd succeed and in the old days, the control was downright spooky. Democratic Party bosses like Chicago's Richard Daley, the elder, had his hand on the throat of city politics for a good long time. Daley was a powerful politician, the likes of which we have not witnessed since he passed from the scene. Today's political hacks have nothing on the men of old. This is cause for great optimism, despite spin machines and angry, destructive shouting.

Fear mongering and name calling needs to settle down a bit in order to return civil dialogue to some measure of sanity. Angry pundits want citizens to believe all liberals are bent on fulfilling Karl Marx's pledge to destroy Capitalism. We have to understand that getting beyond hateful rhetoric shouted by moronic voices advocating ignorance will take time. The alternative is the destruction of dissent. Even positive symbols can be perverted into something mean and purposeless when taken too far.

The lapel pin became a symbol of patriotism after September 11, 2001. It showed pride, a sense of honor, and remembrance. It soon morphed into an insignia of self-congratulation. It was meant to show respect and solidarity but it became a distortion of the meaning of the flag. A simple pin turned into a tool to flog opponents if they did not step in line. It is as if the flag lapel pin were a sign of some demented order of self-flagellating priests living in secret dungeons deep below the streets in a forgotten portion of an ancient city; except these acolytes claim to be the people's priests and they have become the scions of angry, vindictive America. They wear their patriotism on their sleeve, as the saying goes, and this makes it hard to feel admiration for their views.

The left is just as angry as the right, they are just not as effective. The attack ad against General Patreus by Move-On, for example, was wrong, not only short-sighted and ineffectual. Disagreeing on the issues is one thing and there was nothing unethical with the content of the ad. But playing with words like betrayal with anyone, let alone a lifelong public servant, is in terrible taste…it is as if someone were to…I don't know…merge a photo of the world's most notorious terrorist with a man who lost his limbs in Viet Nam. The difference…few Republicans denounced the attack ad against Max Cleland.

The amazing part regarding angry leftist groups is many people would never know anything about them if the right wing pundits did not elevate them to some sort of cult status. At the same time, the only real danger coming out of the angry right is their refusal to hold their party of choice accountable for anything.

They are so intently focused on anti-"liberal" attacks, they don't seem to have noticed the failed policies, distorted truths, and outright corruption those they support injected into the government. Both sides need to take a look at how they conduct debate and we have to hold the spokes-people for our own sides responsible for their own negativity.

The Rule of Fear

First of all let me assert my firm belief that the only thing we have to fear is fear itself—namely, unreasoning, unjustified terror which paralyzes needed efforts to convert retreat into advance.[3]

~Franklin Roosevelt, 1933

During the Great Depression, Franklin Roosevelt re-assured a fractured populace and reminded them that they should not live in fear. The country felt the grip of terror without jobs, failure at the federal level to heed their concerns, and the persistence of a defeated idealism looking backward for solutions. This was the anti-government philosophy of Harding, Coolidge, and Hoover…and it proved disastrous.

Many a liberal laments the ascension of George Walker Bush, affectionately known as W, to the leading seat of government. Luckily, that seat passes hands, at most, every ten years. It's hard to place all the blame at his feet for what happened between 2002 and 2008 although he has plenty to answer for once he heads down that dark tunnel toward the light at life's end.

Perpetuating rule of a free country based on fear is one of the most cowardly courses open to a president. Glorifying in the mistrust of countrymen for one another is not something suiting those who work for the people. Protecting the "Homeland" became synonymous with whatever the grand leader thought was important. Damn civil rights, full speed ahead.

We need someone who refuses to give into fear, not one warning of how dangerous the world is, how hard the job is, and why it would be easier if it weren't a democracy. All the tough talk about the "Axis of Evil" and being with or against him makes the president look like a dumb brute to at least 49% of his fellow citizens and many people around the world think he's mad.

Freedom and security are not zero sum goals. Government should do everything possible to protect the country against terrorist attacks. This is pretty standard fare for the White House plate of priorities. However, it is not the only important national need.

The U.S. people need reassurance that political discourse means respect for different outlooks. The forty third president's "cowboy diplomacy" was meant to show his resolve and it was based on no compromise and no effort to find common ground. It is ironic…Jesus admonished John: "he that is not against you is for you."[4]

Bush's perversion, whether or not it was purposeful, surreptitiously supports claims of conservative commentators and those following their lead that liberals are traitors and un-American. All of a sudden, in the United States and abroad, anyone deviating from the strict course of ideological purity determined by the White House and its supporters stands against the country. What a hard pill to swallow for so many

Americans who only want what is best for the nation but who feel poor W swerved drastically off course.

Beware the rule of fear: restricting individual liberty in the name of order. This is the original warning to the republic. Understand that a constant battle wages between freedom and power mongers seeking a society of lambs heading to the slaughter. This is combat which can not be won with anger and resentment. It will only be won with hard work and thoughtful disagreements competing in the marketplace of ideas.

Americans have fought tyranny consistently and if we turn away from individual rights in pursuit of state sponsored despotism, liberty will truly be in danger. The rhetoric of fear also corrodes democracy. We have nothing to fear. There is so much goodness here. Terrorists may attack again and we expect officials to work overtime to deter our enemies but we must be wary of endless warfare and its crippling effects.

One version of precaution is a reality where the "enemy" is always near. Healing and hope are lost in the fog of endless panic upheld by shifting alliances. Creative tensions vanish and one party rules with an iron fist, removing dissent from the patriotic menagerie. And then Stalinist motives never seem so real.

There are those who want us to live in terror for the next fifty years due to the extremist Islamists. These alarmists refuse to acknowledge any possibility of victory in the war on terror so there is no need to talk about what winning might mean. As long as fear motivates the electorate to vote against alternative thinkers, their job is assured and they can sell their office to the highest bidder. We should not let these elected employees dismantle the foundation of our country. This is the road to empire and we must avoid it if we are to continue on the course demanded of a truly great nation.

Lights at the End of a Tunnel

The civilization of New England has been like a beacon lit upon a hill, which, after it has diffused its warmth around, tinges the distant horizon with its glow.[5]

~Alexis De Tocqueville, 1835

An alternative vision of America and its potential gazes into a future built on past successes and avoiding pitfalls of aged failures. I see the return of a nation leading the world in constructing new economic engines both environmentally friendly and mindful of human rights. Then, we can continue living where the flag stands for freedom and economics offer broad opportunity.

America will stand tall through it in spite of some of the leadership. The people of this country are strong and smart and liberty provides its own incentives. The free market will produce the technologies of the future but it will not do it on its own.

What does government do? It helps provide order, it protects the feeble, and it works to assuage conflict. A nation dedicated to greed and pure market principles generates small minds supporting weak spirits. The U.S. has always been a nation of idealism, growth, and recovery. Born into slavery, our ancestors abolished it. When thrown into chaos, America survives and prospers. We can find strength in our philosophical underpinnings if we take the time to look a little closer.

The New York Times, The Wall Street Journal, Time, Newsweek, The National Review, The Weekly Standard, The New Republic, Mother Jones, and a host of other publications prove interest in government and society exists. Talk radio is successful because the populace does care about ideas. These conservative radio guys discovered that folks care immensely about the state of our union. As Americans, we vote more often than any other nation in the world and we are far more diverse. The United States is culturally mixed and still over 100 million people voted in 2000 and the electorate exceeded 120 million in 2004. I actually find this very impressive. There is a lot we can do if we think about it.

Critics of liberalism cite the New Deal as the beginning of the fall into a cradle to grave socialism which squashes liberty and impedes the real provider of freedom, industry. It is true that business is integral to any free republic. However, there are times when business fails to provide assurances against its own shortsighted activities. Franklin Roosevelt's presidency did usher in a swelling of the federal government but it is important to realize this was far from the beginning of the growth of federal power.

The early unifying document, laid out in the Articles of Confederation, proved ineffective. It was a states' rights document. States had power to do whatever they deemed appropriate, including not paying for their fair share of the revolutionary bills. Concern over the Articles escalated within the nation about interstate commerce, paying war bills, foreign treaties, and possible conflict between states. The Articles didn't work but the Constitution centralized authority.

In addition, it all didn't go down as easy as modern people often think it did. As I mentioned earlier, The Constitutional Convention originally was supposed to merely amend the Articles, not come up with an entirely new form of government with greater centralized authority. Some revolutionaries were livid.

Then, the growth of the federal government and the power of the courts expanded with the confirmation of John Marshall as Chief Justice in 1801 and with the Louisiana Purchase, something even Jefferson may have believed was un-Constitutional but this didn't stop him. You see, the expansion of central authority has been ongoing and the only way to reverse this trend is to understand what we have, why certain measures were enacted, and how we want our government to look. It is easy to claim to want to reduce federal influence but then we must discuss how. This is where it gets tricky.

Southern states left the union to protect the right to own other human beings, to combat the industrializing North and to protect state sovereignty. Lincoln fought to preserve the Union (federal power). He did not resolve to free the slaves until well into the conflict.

Rabid abolitionists had been around since long before the founding, but Lincoln was not one. He preferred to allow the South to slowly ease itself from under the burden of slavery. In any case, federal power swelled after war and the establishment of the 13th, 14th, and 15th amendments. Still, the South survived for 100 years more under debilitating and humiliating primacy of that old evil wretch Jim Crow...until the central government stepped in and removed the remaining legal vestiges of an immoral system.

Civil rights are not the only arena where federal authority gained influence out of obvious needs. Abusive free market practices decimated landscapes early thus cultivating wide support for federal protection of national lands. In 1864, President Lincoln established an "inalienable public trust" for Yosemite Valley and the Mariposa Grove of Giant Sequoias. Yellowstone was authorized as the nation's first national park in 1872, Yosemite followed in 1890. The National Park Service, created in 1916, today oversees nearly 400 national parks and monuments. The mandate for the Park Service is to assure that these areas and monuments exist for future use by all Americans.[6]

The Forest Service began as a national reserve system created at the end of the 19th century to protect forested lands from the adverse affects of speculators, land grabbers, and large companies profiting from short sighted forest destruction, especially in the West. Land rape was the rule in the late 19th century, not the exception.

Teddy Roosevelt loved and respected nature and he was instrumental in directing the process of protecting our natural heritage before and after he became president. He believed the outdoors was essential in the development of strong minds and bodies and he revered God's creation for its spiritual blessings.

The land is a critical component of who we are and there needs to be a process to manage it for the long term and for the good of all the people, not a privileged few. Laws regulate businesses to protect the land and, in some cases, to keep modern technology away from it, such as in wilderness areas.

Today's laws and bureaucratic structure evolved over two centuries of turmoil, compromise, and (believe it or not) growth. Teddy Roosevelt was known as a trust buster for many of the same reasons people are upset over the corporate culture we experience in our own day. Lynching black folks occurred unabated from the Civil War until well into the 1960s. The treatment of Native Americans surpassed the criminal...treaty violations were the norm. Unfair treatment of workers and women generated the need for someone to do something. In each case, central authority grew in relation to real needs.

Conservatives are fond of attacking liberals for espousing "revisionist history". However, peering into the darkness of the soul makes a person stronger, not weaker. The same can be said of nations. Running away from reality by claiming nothing unjust or deceitful has ever been done in America is true revisionism. A complete analysis of who we are as a nation requires asking hard questions and seeking the facts, not some watered down version hiding our scars and asserting our moral purity. The United States is on a historic mission to become better, stronger, and freer. Past ignorance and false pride can only stand in the way of destiny when people refuse to look at the nation as it is and has been.

The roaring twenties was a time of excess and no conscquences tragically ending in the Great Depression. Franklin Roosevelt enacted an unprecedented number of reforms—the great expansion of the state—which made investment safer, guaranteed bank solvency, and created Social Security.

The absence of federal involvement in the economy left people destitute and still the leadership of the 1920s refused to consider action. Coolidge and Hoover were both good men, well educated, and dedicated to the betterment of humanity and society, but they believed so strongly in the free market that FDR was carried into the White House on a golden throne, his promises to act garnering him praise among the masses. Systemic restructuring made the pursuit of happiness less onerous and provided a safety net for the vast majority of the people.

The turbulent 1960s brought greater modification in the form of civil rights legislation and Lyndon Johnson's Great Society. Like recent times, Johnson presided over an unpopular war with the support of both houses of Congress under his party's control. (Who said "absolute power corrupts absolutely?")[7] Johnson's demons brought him to his knees. He was petty and vulgar with an unquenchable thirst for intrigue and yet he saw injustice and he got civil rights legislation passed. But he went too far with other social welfare programs and the reaction against it has been strong and sustained.

The conservative revolution has many seeds. Richard Nixon would not be considered conservative enough in the modern world. Even Goldwater, who supported individual rights later in his life, would rub many of today's conservatives the wrong way, like his protégé John McCain. And so it goes.

Government growth is attacked at all levels but no one does anything to limit the size of government and return the country to the good old days where men were men and the feds stayed off their backs.

All the reform, restructuring, and centralization means many things: someone laid off has help getting by until she can find another job; there is security in knowing the banks are safe places for life savings; the elderly can live out the end of their days with dignity; a public school system is filled with caring, patriotic men and women dedicating their lives to educating the young, (even those who don't want to pay taxes for public education receive benefits by having a safer society); our environment is on the road to health; companies can't just dump toxins into a river or lake that affects those downstream without fearing some consequences; workers have rights; separate water fountains don't exist; laws regulate restaurants and public areas for cleanliness; education is getting better for Native Americans living on reservations; a woman or a black man have the chance to be president; the water is cleaner, the air less filthy, and the knowledge of nature and the human relationship with it has grown exponentially since those original preservationists fought to establish federally protected areas.

Alas, however, there are still issues the country must face...no one fixes it all. The modern challenge is based in the tug-of-war between priorities. Liberal efforts in the past have, on the whole, been successful, but there is a lot to the ideas of individual responsibility, limited government, and low taxes. Balance is crucial.

Neither workers nor business owners want to be taxed into non-existence, but corporations have to pay their fair share. Schools need work, the environment needs work, roads need work, retirement and healthcare systems need work. At the same time, regulations can be burdensome and overbearing. Balance is essential.

President Clinton proclaimed "the era of big government is over".[9] Clinton and a Republican Congress did a lot to restore trust and confidence in government. This is what we need to look for in our federal representatives…officials willing to work hard and to evaluate programs with all factions at the proverbial "table."

Unfortunately, once the Republican Party got it all, they created an era of rampant spending and ideologically driven management, leaving the country in a large hole. Each side needs to fight the good fight but in order to reduce the size of the federal government and make the whole thing work, there must be a realization of the desire for some government.

In the course of moving a nation, it is important to be realistic. Eliminating popular programs means officials will strive like Sisyphus, the Greek phantom pushing the boulder up the hill which would invariably roll back down as his eternal punishment. But, that is neither here nor there. Assuming local control and limited government are the goals, the debate is over how to get there.

So take up the conservative or liberal mantle or Libertarian or Green. Intelligently and thoughtfully prod social change. Active and engaged citizenship generates creative and exciting possibilities. Believe strongly in the United States of America. The future is bright and we should all be looking forward to being involved in whatever it brings while, at the same time, seeking the wisdom of the past to act as a guide.

A wide range of accomplishments line the halls of United States history. It is hard to comprehend, once you think of it, how folks can feel so disempowered and how "the end is near" mentality has taken such a firm control of the American mind. There is nothing the people of this country can not do, especially once it gets beyond the crisis outlook and the short term gain thinking that has been dominating our culture.

From this land emerged an endless list of heroes: George and Martha Washington, Betsy Ross, John and Abigail Adams, Thomas Jefferson, Sally Hemmings, Louis and Clark, Sacagawea, Johnny Appleseed, Daniel Boone, a host of committed abolitionists, Abraham Lincoln, Frederick Douglas, Harriet Tubman, Crazy Horse, Sitting

Bull, Chief Joseph, Susan B Anthony, W.E.B. Dubois, the suffragettes, The Roosevelts, The Kennedys, Huey Newton, Malcolm X, and Martin Luther King Jr. And the list could go on and on and on. Our nation has also experienced its share of demons but this roll seems so small in comparison.

A catalog of such greatness, diversity, and passion should inform all of us of the potential our structure allows us to realize. It ought to remind us of the awesome power of liberty and it can show us of the opportunities available if we find within the system the recipe for political nobility.

Chapter Four: Security

Walls and Weapons

Complaints are everywhere heard from our most considerate and virtuous citizens...that measures are too often decided, not according to the rules of justice and the rights of the minor party, but by the superior force of an interested and overbearing majority.[1]

~James Madison: Federalist #10, 1788

Homeland Security is the new name. A massive bureaucracy built on an Orwellian prototype. Walls surrounding eerily shadowed figures suggesting the death knell of greatness and freedom. Money flows freely into its coffers. It is a giant, bi-partisan ogre who will never go away. It gives money to Wyoming for chemical suits[2] and buys Utah ATVs and snowmobiles.[3] A million here or there really doesn't amount to much in the pursuit of safety and order. The problem is these things well within the interior don't do much to deter masochistic villains with a bloodlust for God and a penchant for chasing virgins in the kingdom any more than arming them in the 1980s did.

Security is more than order. It arises out of the belief in what is right. It includes physical safety but it reaches deep into the social fabric. Security is: caring for the poor efficiently and effectively, self reliance for energy, oversight of massive polluters, and a strong economy. To some, it is security from governmental interference while others think it is freedom from crime and instability. Still others believe security is the freedom to make of life what they want. There are arguments proposing that the nation will never be secure without warfare while others hope the extinction of conflict will engender a safer world. Whatever one's ideals, it is true that the strength of the whole is critical for the individual.

In a fortress the king and court feel perfectly safe within the inner walls because they are sheltered from knowing about the crumbling outer walls. When the wealthy govern with arrogance and greed, the wall's guardians begin to feel as if they are relegated to the ash heap and their purpose is only to support the lavish lifestyles gracing the royal chambers. Due to the ignorance fostered within and without, the outer walls will, one day, give way and weakness will let enemies spread misery and blight throughout the land. The breakdown begins at the outer edges of any society. It is a constant battle to strengthen the walls through educating those guarding the gates and showing them their lives are worth the weight of a king.

In the United States, even the President works for the citizens. Too often the imperial presidency and an inflated sense of privilege for the overseers demote citizens to the role of subjects and this is undemocratic. We all need to foster a greater awareness of citizen ownership of the state. A secure nation incorporates citizens who are well educated, courageous, and cared for. A wise nation does not measure safety only through its ability and blind enthusiasm to use force but by its compassion and understanding.

Real security comes when we prepare to weather storms so that we come through intact. Material possessions can be rebuilt. The minds and hearts and souls of Americans need to learn again how to yearn to be free. When all the people are strong, safe, and healthy, no bomb can scare us into giving liberty away and no act of terror will generate real fear. Courage comes not only from weapons and, in reality, safety can be undermined if the only thing we believe in is military capacity.

This is not to say elimination of weapons and war are realistic or that relaxing national defenses creates some utopian civilization administered by Platonic noble guardians. Unfortunately, accusations of this kind are leveled against anyone arguing for restriction of the security state and limitation of police powers. The United States led the world by creating international agreements and organizations and establishing avenues of diplomacy after being dragged into two European wars. Policies like pre-emption empty the strongbox of goodwill erected over decades of piloting global relations and this tends to foster scorn and mistrust, creating more work in the long run to rebuild our tarnished relationships and to revitalize international respect for our place in the world.

We have to beware passions for endless warfare which generate self fulfilling prophecies. Organized crime bosses live in darkness due to past injustice, waiting for the return of the one harmed individual willing to take revenge through violence or turning state evidence. The same is true at the level of states because actions don't exist in a vacuum. They have consequences and an overwhelming reliance on warfare and hostility offer poor long term solutions. Examples throughout history and literature show us how acts of brutality and bloodshed return to haunt aggressors and we should be mindful of ancient insight.

Parables teach us how malicious experiments undertaken to avoid perceived dangers frequently end up poorly. In ancient Greece, Laius, the king of Thebes had a son but it was foretold this child would kill his father and marry his mother, Jocasta. Laius, wishing to avoid this fate, sends the child off with a servant to kill him but the servant takes pity and hangs the lad from a tree branch. A bizarre thing to do in the name of mercy but there it is.

The child, Oedipus, is found by a servant from a distant kingdom who takes him to be raised by his king. Oedipus grows up and eventually passes back through Thebes. He meets Laius on the road. Without knowing each other, the two men argue and Oedipus kills Laius. He then heads into town and defeats a monster threatening locals, gaining him the hand of the queen, his mother. Once the truth is discovered (thanks to the servant who hung him up to save him) Jocasta kills herself, Oedipus stabs his own eyes out and wanders the land aimlessly, and their children all die horrible deaths resulting from various quests for power.[4]

In a second story from ancient Greece, Agamemnon proclaims himself commander of all Greeks and he gathers leaders from all the islands together to help his brother, Menelaus, get his wife Helen back from Troy. Ready to sail, problems arise from plague and no wind which cripples the Greek fleet. Somehow, Agamemnon had angered the gods in some way, most likely through his own pride.

Anyway, the only way to get the Gods off the Greek's back was for the king to sacrifice his own daughter, Iphigeneia. He likes his command and has a craving for war so he kills his daughter. The winds pick up and the Greeks are on their way to a ten year adventure. He's an arrogant man but he makes it through the Trojan War alright and heads home, only to be stabbed to death by his wife, Clytemnestra, who has taken another lover and is still enraged at the murder of her daughter. Who can blame her?[5]

These stories underscore basic, timeless human wisdom teaching us in every action there is a reaction...poor judgment and short sighted goals pay us back in time. It may take a generation or more but immorality and injustice do not win in the end.

Our actions in modern times prove to be no different. The U.S. assisted in the overthrow of the elected leader Mosadeq in Iran in the 1950s and we feel the effects to this day. We armed the "freedom fighters" in Afghanistan in the 1980s who eventually morphed into the Taliban who supported Bin Laden and the 19 cowards who hi-jacked planes in September, 2001. It is amazing how reticent we can be to helping other nations build schools while we support every effort to distribute arms as if the cycle of violence somehow makes us more secure. Aggression does not provide a refuge. As the Good Book says, there is a time for war but it also reminds us there is a time for peace. We would do well to work on turning global "swords into plowshares" and re-fashioning at least some of the vast number of "spears into pruning hooks."[6]

Bread and Circuses

Why level downward to our dullest perception always, and praise that as common sense?[7]

~Henry David Thoreau, 1854

The phrase "bread and circuses" explains the Roman efforts to pacify the populace with food and games. By giving the citizens bread, emperors took their minds off of freedom and gladiator contests amused them, pacifying any rebellious notions. It may do us well to be aware of the modern corollary to this. We are offered "bread" in the form of cheap, foreign manufactured goods and our "circus" is television.

In the 1960's, Lyndon Johnson's "Great Society" gave away too much in the form of expensive social programs while creating the circus that was Viet-Nam. That story, however, has been overplayed. Too much time has passed, too much energy has been spent analyzing every nuance of each moment from John Kennedy's assassination on November 23, 1963 to Richard Nixon's departure from the White House on August 18, 1974. It is an old, tired argument but it affects us to this day. There was a lot of rage in the 1960s. It was far from Peace and Love...no matter what they said back in 1967 or how the flashbacks look today.

The public was so worn out by it all Richard Nixon was re-elected in one of the largest landslides in the nation's history in 1972. But he was just too ignorant and paranoid to see it. His pain and terror must have been excruciating once he decided to get back into what he perceived as the brutal, selfish, and corrupt world of national politics in 1968, especially before Bobby Kennedy was shot.

The prospect of losing to another Kennedy must have menaced Richard Nixon's mental capacities. He had gone through a lot in his long political career. He was forced to go on national television in 1952 to deny fiscal improprieties in order to be Dwight Eisenhower's vice-president, claiming the only thing he ever got from public service was his little dog Checkers. He lost to Bobby's brother by one of the smallest margins ever in 1960 which was followed by a defeat in the governor's race in California. Nixon left politics after that loss, swearing no one would kick him around anymore. The opportunity of national power, however, was apparently too great for him to deny.

Nixon must have loathed the Kennedys. All of them. He believed they were uppity, blue blood Northeasterners...he may not have been all that far from the mark. However, we will never know what sort of leaders either of the middle Kennedy brothers may have been in the long haul. We do know they have been lionized and their deaths were tragic moments marking chaotic times while Richard Nixon went down in flames. He was a crook so suspicious he abused his office and he felt he was above the law.

In 1968, Richard Nixon won the presidency by another narrow margin against an old time Democratic Machine Thug, Lyndon Johnson's Vice President Hubert Humphrey. Squeaking by in this way probably started the downfall of a presidency. His paranoia had reached such heights that his storm troopers with the Committee to Re-elect the President (CREEP) were given enough rope to hang over the White House rafters.

It is important to remember that political memories are long and clear. Nixonian acolytes returned the favor for what they perceived was injustice for poor Richard and in 1998 they attacked Bill Clinton with a ferocity unseen in the divisive times before or since. The GOP controlled Congress and they smelled blood. They couldn't find much but that didn't even slow them down. In the end: Nixon left with 24% approval rating while Clinton left office intact with 65% of the public approving of his work.[8] And so it goes.

The lessons of history aren't hard to follow. The past is filled with men and women believing they were above the law and getting their due in the end. We have to travel beyond the myth of economics and freedom which justify the notions that it is all-important to be able to buy lots of poorly made stuff and a nice TV. Our consumer orientation leads us into carelessness which threatens our economic strength. We are often told not to think of where or how our purchases are made. China and India will someday have thriving middle classes and they won't always have the need for the U.S. market. What will we do then? We too often get distracted by the political games instead of reflecting on the successes of the past and looking forward with an appreciation for our nation and its strengths.

Corporate Welfare and the Fleeting Bliss of Ignorance

"Are there no prisons?" asked Scrooge.
"Plenty of prisons," said the gentleman, laying down the pen again.
"And the Union workhouses?" demanded Scrooge. "Are they still in operation?"
"They are. Still," returned the gentleman, "I wish I could say they were not."
"The Treadmill and the Poor Law are in full vigour, then?" said Scrooge.
"Both very busy, sir."
"Oh! I was afraid, from what you said at first, that something had occurred to stop them in their useful course," said Scrooge. "I'm very glad to hear it."[9]

~Charles Dickens, 1843

Everyone knows Ebenezer Scrooge. Each Christmas he reminds us life is more than profit and business. Supply side economics assures us if we reduce requirements on the wealthy they will invest and spend money and raise the standard of living for the rest of us. The upper class, however, demand a great deal from the rest of society. For all their protestations of unfairness arrayed against them it is difficult to know where a just line between staying off their backs while getting them to help take care of the bills when they come due.

Dickens does not argue against capitalism but he points out that unconstrained love of profit is de-humanizing. When Scrooge learns the error of his ways he does not give up his business. He simply partakes in the human drama more fully and he learns how his narrow view kept him away from understanding the whole truth of life.

Revolution arrives when the poor have simply had enough. Rosa Parks was just too darn tired that day. Injustice and inequity wear on the human spirit. At the same time, supposed free marketeers demand governmental subsidies and then have the gall to call themselves conservatives at cocktail parties.

This is a major problem with our debates today. We do not think hard enough about the true differences in the two major philosophies directing our decision making processes. This is how catchphrases make their way into the headlines and the end result is that we fail to govern ourselves with care and competence and it just depends upon which large organization wins the ability to direct our resources.

The United States spends more time concerning itself with tax shelters instead of homeless and battered women's shelters. The truth is that some things lie outside the market and these are the things government should be involved in and these things have a cost associated with them. Ignoring poverty while using social power to advance the interests of the rich won't enhance freedom and it can destabilize the population.

Reducing the size and scope of the federal government requires elected officials to stop pandering to corporate interests and upholding failed endeavors. At the same time, it is important to support entrepreneurial initiatives by combining incentives with pragmatic risk assessments. It also is necessary to involve industry in cultivating solutions, turning ideas into action. Divorcing capitalism, profit, and growth from ethics deprives us of meaningful alternatives, forcing authority into the hands of privacy advocates and increasing opportunities for corruption.

Privatization of all services is misguided— it leads to greater regulation and control over the long term because people clamor form assistance when businesses fail and individuals are harmed. Arguments over regulation and free economics are not easy but we need substantive discussions about how we deal with big industry in the global age.

There is no question people who work hard deserve to keep the fruits of their labor, their earnings. Capitalism and freedom are intertwined, connected at the hip yet unfettered business practices do not raise standards of living, protect workers, and keep the environment clean. In short, government is necessary to engender true security because corporations will not do so on their own.

Much of the income generated in America comes from good roads, stable infrastructure, educated citizens willing to work, and a healthy natural world allowing workers to rejuvenate thus raising productivity. Industry generates a great deal of waste which society deals with in it landfills.

On the other hand, many industry leaders have learned it is in their interest to "reduce, reuse, and recycle". The throwaway society is dying, breathing its last breaths, and its demise will make America more secure. Industry should lead the way in crafting solutions for the twenty first century but too often, they refuse because our entire mindset is guided by selling everything out for short term gain and government too often helps to uphold this fragile, dated economics.

The security of the nation depends on many things lying outside the marketplace. Throwing money at problems doesn't fix them, but neither does ignoring them and hoping they go away. Some things have a price tag and it is important for elected officials to learn how to pay for things desired by the citizens. The focus on relentless tax cuts instead of a greater emphasis on tax equity is advantageous to the corporate bottom line at the expense of the country as a whole. The reality is that the inability or unwillingness to understand what government should do inhibits the free market.

There is such a tremendous siege mentality covering business relations in the United States and the conflict paradigm benefits the status quo. Corporate irresponsibility and tax incentives to move overseas or to conduct business without considering environmental or human consequences costs more money over time but businesses have clout and they demand incentives for short term gain. This will not keep the country safe and prosperous over the long term.

Prison

Under a government which imprisons any unjustly, the true place for a just man is also a prison.[10]

~Henry David Thoreau, 1849[10]

Personal responsibility can not be overstated. Law and order are vital but the extreme number of prisoners highlights social failures. When states have to let people out early and whole economies rely on prisons to uphold their existence, we have to think about reform. We are not a nation of criminals and thugs and somehow we must figure out how to encourage the youth to take responsibility for their actions while reducing crime.

America has a growing love affair with prisons. The incarcerated population has grown to epic proportions. This nation has a higher prison population per capita compared with any other nation in the world. What does this say about national security? The drug war is an unmitigated failure and police powers reach into the heart of the country to drag down inner city youth with reckless abandon. Protection from crime is important for people's feelings of safety but the way we are headed, it is unsustainable. Prisons are overcrowded, bursting at the seams. One answer is privatization.

However, prisons are not a function of the market. Government out-sources the job of building and maintaining prisons to profiteers and these functionaries act with impunity regarding funding. Privatized prisons form a perverse incentive to fill up the beds. How will the government get out of the prison business if it ever figures out the importance of well built schools and better pay for teachers which may make a dent in criminal activity if serious profit is involved?

And what happens if the people actually speak up for common sense and decriminalize marijuana so vast numbers of prisoners on petty drug offences are set to go free? Who pays for the private industry which has opened up around prisons? The public does. The point here is to emphasize how privatization is not truly an anti-government ideology but one which simply alters the power structure and costs more in the end without dealing effectively with our criminal population.

Non-violent criminals need not be locked up for extended periods of time. Over two million people reside within the prison system. We should focus on teaching the vitality and promise of our nation and laws which may build respect for the system and for other people. Prison is often simply punishment, cruel and degrading at times, dull and ignorant at others. It's hard to see how this truly benefits the rest of us.

Prison is most definitely a security issue. Ask anyone who has been robbed, beaten, raped, or had a loved one murdered. Ask people who are afraid to leave their homes. Victim's rights are central to any measure aimed at prison restructuring. There is no reason a murderer or sex offender should be released onto the streets early.

The argument that greater enforcement is the only remedy protecting innocents is compelling. However, reducing the number of activities society deems criminal while utilizing alternative measures of oversight of drug offenders keeps more beds open for violent criminals, keeping them locked up where they should be. At the same time we absolutely must take these numbers as a warning and a call to provide substantive education and to create hope among our young people.

Anytime something is institutionalized it becomes difficult to modify it. Alter it in any way and you'll be taking on those in control. The larger the prison system, the closer we come to a police state. The prison issue is bipartisan. Incarceration numbers increased during Republican and Democratic control. Neither party reduces the number of jailbirds. Republicans don't believe in it and Democrats fear more Willie Horton ads.

The point of all this is not to argue we need to tear down the prison walls, but to say we must emphasize education, infrastructure, and to figure out how to revitalize inner cities. It would be nice to see the leadership working together. Republicans are correct about empowerment generating pride but helping poorer folks also benefits the general welfare.

Imagine if we spent money on inner cities, if business invested more there, if low cost condominium complexes replaced aging, destructive projects and urban enterprise zones provided greater ownership. These efforts would reduce the long term prison population and be an investment in a safer place now and for tomorrow. The benefits would be far reaching. Ideas exist on both sides of the political aisle but it takes serious discussions to implement any form of restructuring.

It is also time to end modern prohibition. Decriminalizing marijuana, at the very least, will reduce the hold on society the prison system has gained and reduce illegal activity just like repealing alcohol prohibition did in the 1930s. How many good and decent people spent time behind bars for possession of a plant?

We are living in an age which has been created by the past. It took ninety years and a bloody war to offer freedom to black folks and another hundred years of terror before any semblance of rights was grudgingly secured. Native Americans waged plenty of war with each other, but the U.S. government continuously broke treaties, stole land, and spit on the rights and dignity of Natives. John Brown, a revolutionary abolitionist, knew blood would spill in the name of the righteousness of God and against the heathen Southern system.

Not to be outdone by the South and its errant ways, Northern politicos and society in general supported building ghettos for blacks and they kept a heel on the backs of blacks while shaking hands publicly and declaring their own upright standing and moral superiority to the South in race relations.

Throughout our history, protestors gathering for workers rights were beaten, our waterways polluted, our forests decimated, 4 little girls were blown up and 4 students were shot. Civil rights organizations have been targeted as terrorists and put on watch lists by shadowy figures governed by no one at all. And we wonder where the origins of crime comes from!

All of this historical baggage lay just below the surface, tearing at the social fabric. While "Leave it to Beaver" played to an audience of God fearing Americans, a storm was brewing. We always live with the consequences of our own ignorance. There is a lot of historical injustice we are striving to move beyond.

This is not an apology for criminals. Harm to others is never justified unless in self defense, lawbreakers should be accountable, and personal responsibility is important. The glorification of violence in Hollywood and in the music industry does no one any good but we demand the freedom of expression. We need to stop glorifying violence, anger, and crime and, at the same time, we need to learn from history about the roots of criminal activity. Then we can continue to move in a more positive direction.

We have come a long way from fearing nothing but fear. Every corner turned and every step taken brings calls of caution and people are advised to look over their neighbor's shoulders. Is that really security? It is certainly not freedom. The world is uncertain and perilous but to be consumed with passion and irrational angst against all dangers great and small means we have given up the fight and forgotten our core values. Perhaps we need to teach these more fully.

Chapter Five: Civil Rights and the American Way

Civil Rights

They came first for the Communists,
and I didn't speak up because I wasn't a Communist.
Then they came for the Jews,
and I didn't speak up because I wasn't a Jew.
Then they came for the trade unionists,
and I didn't speak up because I wasn't a trade unionist.
Then they came for the Catholics,
and I didn't speak up because I was a Protestant.
Then they came for me –
and by that time no one was left to speak up for me.[1]

~Pastor Martin Niemoller, circa 1946

Pastor Niemoller presented a reminder of how precious civil rights are and how precarious they can be. A safe and free society upholds justice, not simply retribution. Today it is easy to disregard and forego talk of civil rights but civil rights are not charming remnants of a long forgotten past. They are the means by which our country thrives. They illustrate the importance of democracy and they highlight the transformative capabilities of politics.

Unfortunately, in a time where order takes precedence, personal autonomy is placed on the back burner. Civil rights don't provide a license for disrespect. Reverence for the nation, however, needs to be met with deference from the establishment for the rights of the individual. It is easy, like Niemoller, to ignore civil rights until it is you backed into the corner facing brutality at the hands of those sworn to protect and serve. In any democracy there is a constant tension between the individual and the state. This is an important aspect of democratic order. Today, the state is winning because we seem to have forgotten about the importance of our rights.

Protecting average people from the ruling class is what civil rights are all about. Why else would the First Amendment provide protections for speech, the press, religion, and assembly? These protections are not thoughtless phrases added to fill space. They are the product of discussion, debate, and experience and they keep things in balance. Every time the winds of change rip at the fabric of the sails of the ship of state, America arrives at a distant shore weary but unshaken thanks to the works of our founders. Freedom to dissent is vital.

Civil rights make the U.S. the envy of humanity. There is always a need to strive for expanding free will and opportunity for all. It is not perfect...never has been. It can be refined though and each generation must assert its commitment to the rights of all. This fuels the signal of freedom so encouraging to the rest of the world.

James Madison was concerned with minority rights. He wasn't so concerned with the rights of racial minorities important in the twenty-first century; his slaves would probably have testified he had little concern for their rights back in the day. He was concerned with the rights of the political minority, including those rights steamrolled by a majority of the citizens when 51 per cent determines the fate of the nation. It is these political rights, codified in our Constitution, which forms the groundwork upon which all other civil rights battles have been waged and won.

Today, dire warnings fill the airwaves about giving gays the right to marry. Then, of course, there will be trouble. Why? Who knows? Don't ask questions! It is downright un-American. Now really, most people don't care one way or another. They may be a bit spooked about the whole legitimacy of marriage thing but we gave up on this concept when the divorce rate started climbing so steadily. I find it dubious at best to believe that gay marriage will have anything to do with the destruction of the United States of America.

It is true, in 1903, just about everyone stayed married. It is also true that at this earlier, simpler time, no one discussed domestic violence, recognized child abuse or sexual predators, or considered lynching (except spooky cowards in bed sheets chanting in clearings to the light of burning symbols of God). People should be left alone to love who they wish and love should be what society holds up to a standard. Love needs no government oversight so we need no law relating to it.

Concerning a Constitutional Amendment against gay marriage, it is sad to think some are willing to amend the founding document in opposition to the rights of individuals. The government does not need to regulate morality. It is funny how so many people who supposedly desire small government want to use police powers to control private, individual, moral decisions. I find it odd.

Marriage is a foundation of society, but perhaps we should examine this idea in relation to history. How many teenage slave girls gave birth to children of the "noble" class? How many married individuals in the modern world conveniently provide distance between themselves and their wedding vows? This is not an assault on marriage. Marriage should be forever but it does not require stringent government oversight.

If society holds love up to the level as marriage nothing can destroy it. There are no storms a married couple can't weather if they have faith in each other and if they truly love each other. This, it seems, should be the standard of marriage. In any case, freedom is the ability to choose how you want to live your life as long as you don't harm others. This is the true meaning of civil rights and liberties.

The Welfare State

There is nothing new about poverty. What is new is that we now have the techniques and the resources to get rid of poverty. The real question is whether we have the will.[2]

~Martin Luther King Jr., 1968

The federal government should have a role in assuring full employment and in making sure opportunities are open to workers at the bottom of the economic scale. Welfare to work seems logical— paying men and women to learn skills while giving back to the country can not be a bad example to set for the youth and it can give a great deal of hope to the hopeless. In the wasted years of the Great Depression, men were put to work by the Civilian Conservation Corps created by Franklin Roosevelt's administration. These men restored land, provided necessary services the market could not provide, and earned a living wage. This helped build pride and it gave people a sense of self sufficiency. This is a far better use of tax dollars than no-bid contracts given to the well connected.

Cooperation and conciliation reformed the welfare system and we all need to acknowledge the successes of past leadership while seeking further adjustments to our policy choices which will enhance our ability to confront the future. Conflict over intricate federal issues can generate results if we are willing to stand up for our beliefs and still learn from the art of compromise. This is not to say we desire a welfare nation or a socialist trajectory. It is to notice we live in a new century which brings with it possibilities as well as obstacles.

We are lost without a sense of direction but we are hopeless without an appreciation for the choices this society has made in the past. Poverty is a terrible disease and if we dream large enough, we may be able to solve the most pressing social needs. The alleviation of poverty does not mean the onslaught of governmental oppression and the death of capitalism. It will only make our nation and economy stronger.

So many gifted, intelligent young people yearn for opportunity. Why should the nation turn its collective back on them and give them a hearty "good luck, pull yourself up by your bootstraps." Dead end roads lead to endless forms of misery and crime.

There are no loopholes for the poor and the downtrodden, only a void where people lose all hope as they struggle to exist in an arena of bleak, utter darkness. Forty years after Martin Luther King Jr. asked the people of this nation to think of the poor, millions of our fellow citizens live in poverty. Children in this country lay their heads down in a place they can not call home every day. We should be able to talk about these facts without being attacked. It is not mindless liberalism but compassionate patriotism.

Charles Dickens wrote lucid accounts of the blight and extreme conditions wrought from the unhindered quest of the dollar in the nineteenth century. Have we learned so little to this day?

It is important to know if we think we should return to the late 1800s or if we should march grandly into our own century. We don't need a larger, more powerful central government. We do need thoughtful and considered proposals which acknowledge the needs of all of our people.

What is a Living Wage?

No business which depends for existence on paying less than living wages to its workers has any right to continue in this country.[3]

~Franklin D. Roosevelt, 1933

Violence erupts in oppressed communities as a result of despair. Hopelessness breeds contempt for others, especially those of wealth and privilege. It is difficult for people earning $20,000 per year to raise a family. Assuring living wages is a family value. Millions of families barely make it through the day with what they earn. Concern for the working poor is among the most pressing issues facing us. 45 million people have no health insurance and when cost of health care and poor education gets factored into any equation of wealth, these issues affect current children and will pressure their children's children.

There are no easy answers to the quandary of decent wages with benefits. Those who want to turn back the clock to a simpler time are living a fantasy. If you argue the market is the best way to move into the future, fine but a quick glance backwards exhibits glaring examples of the market gone bad, leaving millions to fend for themselves against powerful odds.

It is not Socialist to consider market failures relating to health care, work, and education. Different solutions are conceivable so again we need honest debate, not simplistic slogans entrenched in ideology. If privatization is the option, why are there problems today? The implications of privatization are enormous considering millions of Americans rely on Medicaid, Medicare, Social Security, and other state run programs. There are American citizens living day to day in fear of the coming health disaster which may force them into poverty. State run programs can be combined with personal responsibility and the result would be far healthier than the current reality.

In the wealthiest, most powerful nation in history, is it OK for children to go hungry or to live without adequate education? Is it OK when patients lack insurance? Problems arise out of government funded healthcare and these are seen in Canada, Britain, and France, but all we need to do is create a uniquely American future.

There should be national shame when a parent working two jobs and raising children can't afford medication, when emergency rooms are clogged because they are the only avenue for care to those without insurance or when the elderly live in poverty. Yet there is such a faith in low tax rates we turn away from these issues. Callousness will not create stability.

In the past, children worked and the argument abounded—it was a cold, cruel world, so deal with it. Our ancestors ended child labor through law and political will. The federal government has tried and succeeded to reduce a bit of the hardship causing anguish and despair. Is this so wrong? We in this country believe "all [people] are created equal and [we] are endowed by our Creator with certain inalienable rights. That among these rights are life, liberty, and the pursuit of happiness."[4] Civil rights are those guaranteed by the government. These can include health care, employment insurance, some form of assistance for children in need, and the right to enjoy the freedom of nature without being socialism.

Chapter Six: Fiscal Responsibility

Deficits and Wealth

Bankruptcy and repudiation are the springboards from which much of our civilization vaults and turns its somersets.[1]
~Henry David Thoreau, 1854

Increased deficits, rising poverty, and reduced average wage levels show how easy it is to sell out to the lowest bidder. At the same time, the leadership tells us everything is fine and the economy is fundamentally sound. It is not hard to argue that their analysis is fundamentally flawed. This did not start as a corporate country and we should not settle for it now.

Government failures can be enormous but the free market only works with parameters in place protecting the general health and welfare. Heavy debt burdens the nation. On the other hand, Alan Greenspan worried over abusive federal manipulation if officials had a big surplus in their greedy little hands.[2] He wrote this would create the incentive to artificially interfere with market processes. There is no pleasing the economists. But whatever fears he had were put to bed between 2001 and 2008 as the national debt soared out of control.

Borrowing is no new vice and it has some benefits. Back in the day Adams, Franklin, and Jefferson, among others, traveled across the Atlantic to see who would loan our new nation badly needed capital. Long term reliance upon borrowing is another story. The nation never pays down its current debts before racking up new, grander obligations. At the same time, we have been told for thirty years that entitlement spending will crush us all. It is a long term war waged by ideologues to decimate social welfare spending without addressing budget commitments seriously.

The federal government can, in fact, take control of budgets and they can pay down the debts if we demand it. Unfortunately for the Republican Party, once they gained all the muscle, the skids were greased and they collectively imploded like the Soviet Union. The Party was eaten from the inside out like a cancerous growth and they took the nation with them on their downward slide.

Once they got kicked out of the driver's seat for managing like speed freaks, the Democrats took the reigns, maneuvering with a lack of skill and grace which would make President Millard Fillmore proud. The battles between the White House and The Congress in 2007 brought partisan bickering to a new low. Congressional Republicans, meanwhile, supported the president in every stubborn action he assured us was absolutely necessary, as if no one else knows anything of social needs. Meanwhile the Democrats flailed around like fish out of water.

Republicans controlled Congress for twelve years for two reasons. First, during the early years, under the direction of Newt Gingrich, the party made tough choices and helped balance the budget, getting our fiscal house in order. According to all the participants involved, it was not easy. Intense and extensive negotiations with the White House took place which moderated both views. Second, 911 repeated ad infinitum was used as a battle cry to scare voters into supporting the party.

They lost control due to poor decisions involving these very same issues. Fiscal impropriety and neglect of office made voters shake their heads and their tactics designed to elevate public panic and to attack the rest of us who disagree with them made voters think twice about the true dangers facing the nation.

For the second six years, the Republican Congress and President refused to balance budgets, take responsibility for anything, or work with the minority. No compromise was the solution to each and every issue while ignorance and brute force dominated the discourse. Whoever is in power would do well to learn from their lessons if they want to stay in power. Democrats were on the run in 2004 and they would have spent much more time as the minority party had the Republicans not imploded.

Some Democrats even turned on their own...like the weird angry Senator from Georgia, Zell Miller. Miller wanted to duel Hardball's Chris Mathews during the Republican convention.[3] I guess this is just par for the course of American politics. But people have tired of the baseless, cartoon-like anger and endless heated rhetoric aimed at capturing headlines. It reduces our ability to talk to each other over important issues such as wealth, debt, and power.

Current ideological imperatives relating to the terrible "other" group who will destroy the nation leave political dialogue embittered and lost. Then fiscal responsibility is left at the wayside, lost and forgotten in a haze of spite and antagonism. This is why we lose faith in our system which leads to irresponsibility no matter who is in the White House and Congress.

Borrow and Spend Conservatives

Isn't it time we hold Congress accountable for how much they spend— and for what?[4]

~The Republican Party, 1994

The moniker "tax and spend" has been around for a long time now. Elected officials cringe when being labeled a "tax and spend liberal" and they hide in the shadows. Many public employees only show their face on television or on tax payer funded color brochures intended to benefit their re-election. "Tax and spend" has become one more simple slogan with little meaning and it impedes American progress.

Unfortunately, it is difficult in these days to trust ideologically driven tax cuts or subsidies disproportionately benefiting the richest Americans. Big government is no answer. Smaller government that does not tamper with God given, constitutionally ordained civil rights and liberties holds a great deal of promise if people hold their elected officials and multi national corporations who fund them accountable.

The enormous fiscal dereliction of duty has been preposterous. Think tanks now exist to rationalize and promote the ultimate destruction of the federal government. However, Republican rulers were so blind with rage their effectiveness was threatened and their mindless support of poorly thought out policies led them to simply conduct business as usual but to borrow for everything.

It would not be surprising if among those who got us into the mess we're in, some have designs to shove the federal government over the cliff, watching it fail with glee. It is such a tragic tale of excess and irresponsibility, it is hard not to believe in conspiracy theories, otherwise, this group of madmen was simply composed of dumb, irrational brutes caring little for their country and less for its people. Nobody wants to believe this, although many already do.

The sad truth of it all is the reduction of taxes requires a concurrent reduction in services. Perhaps it is true the entire tax structure needs to be scrapped and the project needs to be started over. In the meantime, people like what the federal government provides, whether they proclaim themselves conservative or liberal. It is an amazing reality in modern America.

Conservatives consistently relied upon borrowing in order to avoid tough choices requisite of balanced budgets and fiscal discipline. The lesson available through the period covering 1995 to 2001 is that the government's finances can be balanced and choices can be made but it takes more than some ideological mantra and endless efforts to demonize the opposition. The White House and Congress fought the good fights and the results were an array of impressive policies so voters sent representatives back to work. Smart politics means negotiation, compromise, hard work, and balanced budgets. If either party figures this simple formula out, their future is secure.

It is depressing in so many ways. You know the Democrats are trying to steal your money—but at least then you sometimes get something in return. The Republicans just spent the same money less effectively but they stole it from your grandchildren while telling us it was all in the name of small government and personal responsibility.

There is a theme developing today—conservative ideals are strong and good but when they are perverted through antagonism, deception, and self righteousness, they reveal just another group of swindlers gorging at the public trough. To many of us, it appears that we are debating only which exceedingly wealthy interest groups are the ones who will benefit from governmental policies instead of examining the relationship between strong economics which take account of what we want and need. We can pay for what we need if we practice what we preach and if we choose policies which take account of governmental responsibility while actually discussing what federal programs are important and which work towards supporting social health.

Personal Debt

In a market economy, rising debt goes hand in hand with progress[5]
~Alan Greenspan, 2007

2007 saw the start of the crisis in secondary lending threatening financial institutions and sending shock waves shattering the housing market. The government, under President Bush, stepped in and negotiated a deal with financial institutions relieving pressure on dubious loans affecting everyone from the construction community to Wall Street brokers, unveiling problems with unfettered capitalism. Credit helps people realize their dreams and it allows them to take chances otherwise unavailable to them but once things go too far the effects can be staggering.

Secondary loans carry high risk for loan providers who naturally require higher interest rates. The lending institutions give opportunities to people who would not have a chance to live in their own homes without banks taking a chance on them. The problem arising out of attempts to regulate the banking industry is it will be less likely to make loans to people living on the edge. On the other hand, predatory lending does occur. The difficulty lies in figuring out the correct equation protecting the ignorant while providing opportunity for those who have thought things through.

One thing Congress did was make it harder for individuals to declare bankruptcy. Bankruptcy is so important and its effects have been known for so long, it is written of in the Constitution. What Congress did, however, protected the major credit corporations at the expense of individual borrowers.

The road always winds back around to personal responsibility. Caveat emptor, buyer beware, is the rule of the times. Personal debt needs to be available for those in need of cars, homes, and even to start businesses. There are times when people need money to get by and without secondary lending, all of this ends. The question thus becomes what is the correct balance between economic freedom and responsibility. If the federal government is willing and able to bail out large corporate lenders, why are we so reluctant to assist personal borrowers?

The free market provides wealth to the nation and borrowing is one element helping businesses and elevating education in the lives of many people. People must not let the uncertainty of a moment lead them into rash decisions which, in the end, will harm them when this may be unnecessary. Adam Smith wrote of the vagaries of capitalism and outlined how it would ebb and flow as the market adjusted itself.

Keynesian economics, named after John Meynard Keynes, who worked for Franklin Roosevelt, created a place for government intervention to protect the entire system in lieu of the unstable natural forces at play. This protected individuals and made a stronger system. This is very important to remember in these days where globalism is creating such uncertainty.

This is the balancing act involved in self government, figuring out the delicate relationship between too much regulation and the possibility of tragic human consequences of unhindered economic activity. This is becoming an even greater concern as more of our jobs become intertwined with our global reality. Throughout the coming years, we need to have a real national dialogue about how we wish to shape our economic future. This will greatly affect personal debt and wealth creation.

Market freedoms created the stock market bubble and the housing crisis. Both of these hurt a lot of people. Government needs to effectively address excesses without regulating cash flow out of existence. It is a thin line and a rough one and it is hard to understand why anyone would want the job of the presidency, but there you go.

The unemployment rate has actually been amazingly low for the past few years. Jobs exist for folks willing to work. They may not be the best paying jobs and often they don't include any sort of insurance, but jobs are out there. It seems to me it is an imperative for our society to make sure opportunity exists for those willing to work hard and who will take the steps necessary to provide for their families. Personal debt can be destructive or it can be a foundation to take a chance and to secure funding for alternative business paradigms. Profit motives don't exist only in the highest echelons of the entrepreneurial arena.

The Poor and The Rich

The fruits of the toil of millions are boldly stolen to build up colossal fortunes for a few, unprecedented in the history of mankind; and the possessors of those, in turn despise the Republic and endanger liberty. From the same prolific womb of governmental injustice we breed the two great classes—tramps and millionaires.[6]

~The Populist Party Platform, 1892

The gap between the poor and the rich has been a concern in this country for generations. We have to learn to change our behaviors for the benefit of the entire nation. Business executives realize the need for change. They call it growth. In their view, however, growth is always more: more sales, more business, more money. Growth is never questioned in this universe. It is necessary and good and that's all anyone needs to know. How would it look, though, if we examined the ideas surrounding growth more intimately? We don't need to try and pull the wealthy down but to build a stairway for the poor to walk up.

What would happen if the conceptual framework upholding one of the central tenets of American industry was supplemented with other positive attributes? If growth consisted of more than just the bottom line, how would wealth react? Self interest and community can work together if we are willing to take the leap and create our future instead of just wishing someone would get it together and do something.

Competition and cooperation are not mutually exclusive. Business growth can be tied to social welfare, environmental health, and economic freedom if we can only imagine what is possible instead of dying on the vine of past assumptions. Capitalism works best on long term goals and it generates such hopeful opportunities, it is a shame we rely on outdated notions.

Federal funding assisting the poorest of people strengthens the social fabric. It is necessary for people to educate themselves and work to better their conditions and, yes, to take responsibility for their lives. But government should be there to provide a safety net for those living at the bottom of the economy and for others who have fallen on hard times. Will there always be exploitation? Probably. But is this a reason to give up on all those who need a bit of rope now and then to keep them from plummeting into the abyss?

When the richest nation in history, spending a small portion of its budget on poverty, allows the depravation of its poorest members while supporting multi-billion dollar negotiations taking place on corporate jets with individuals who would sell Alaska for a decent profit, the result is the creation of an indifferent and feeble society.

The poor are not some amorphous collection of vagabonds attacking drivers with window washing equipment. They are fellow citizens and neighbors living among the rest of us. The poor who rely on governmental programs are not getting rich. They are getting by.

The common lament is that taxes are too high and businesses won't run with regulation. What of the conditions in 1929. By the time Franklin Roosevelt was elected people had enough of no government intervention at all costs. Roosevelt took federal action to alleviate poverty and make the private sector stronger so such a disaster would never happen again. And we have not seen anything like it since then.

If there are problems with the welfare system, fine. Write Congress and the President and ask them to fix it further. But we have to consider the implications of poverty. They are real and they have exploded into violence in the past. Even on the pure principles of individualism there is an argument which can be made for programs which aim to reduce poverty intelligently.

What if we created something similar to Roosevelt's Civilian Conservation Corps? Let welfare recipients get out into nature, learn some things about working for something greater than themselves, and provide skills with which they can make a better life when they return to their homes. In return, society gets national park restoration, forest health work, city park upkeep, and rooftop gardens...all at a reasonable cost. There is so much which can be done and it would cost us so little. It seems a shame there is such antipathy towards any sort of ideas of this kind.

We need to realize we are all Americans, no matter what the balance is in our bank accounts. This is not a "soak the rich" philosophy. It is just a call for comprehension about the problems of poverty and the possible consequences of the growing disparity of wealth confronting us. It is illogical to argue the poor should be provided everything from the government but to hide our heads in the sand and ignore daily struggles of our fellow citizens is not a long term answer grounded in facts and it ignores actual assessments of the problems we are facing.

Roosevelt and Perot

There is a widespread conviction in the minds of the American people that the great corporations known as trusts are in certain of their features and tendencies hurtful to the general welfare. This...is based upon sincere conviction that combination and concentration should be, not prohibited, but supervised and within reasonable limits controlled; and in my judgment this conviction is right.[7]

~Theodore Roosevelt, 1901

Third party candidates make a difference in policy and can affect national elections. Theodore Roosevelt, after spending eight years in the White House and four years on the sidelines watching President William Howard Taft ignore his legacy, helped form the Progressive Party and took enough votes from Taft to give Woodrow Wilson the White House in 1912. Roosevelt had originally ascended into the presidency after a worthless psychotic with revolutionary desires shot William McKinley nine months into his second term way back in 1901. Roosevelt was a staunch environmentalist who supported worker's rights, women's rights, child labor laws, limits on corporate influence, and other policies aimed at justice and securing citizen rights and liberties.

Third party candidates focus national attention and the successful ones are built upon citizen priorities. The end result is normally the loss of the main party candidate closest to the third party. It is a strange realm of politics. Candidates run to push the system in a new direction, guide the dialogue, and force the major party politicians to take heed of their warnings.

Ross Perot got people up off the couch to vote for him using charts and graphs to illustrate the monstrosity of national debt. He gathered a substantial portion of the vote in 1992 and forced policy makers to take his movement seriously. It is hard to believe the odd little man wanted to be president at all. He seemed to think a president could just make things happen and he did not appear to value discussion over what he was going to do. Still, Perot showed how the interest on the national debt could be used to pay for houses for everyone west of the Mississippi and he struck a chord with voters. People who never voted before lined up to register and fill in the oval for H. Ross Perot and this is always good for democracy.

Third party candidates can slap the two main contenders around, give a jolt to the rest of us and remind us why we take part in democracy. If they are successful, like Roosevelt and Perot, they generate such a stir that they, along with their supporters, move mountains and change the world.

There are others, like Ralph Nader in 2000, who act merely as spoilers and it is hard to see any good coming out of the act of running but they still build a platform for a fair number of people and this is good. Many people were upset at Nader because he helped elevate a somewhat naïve, good natured ex-partier into the Oval Office but this is what happens in the American political world.

Successful third parties focus our attention on ideas, force accountability and, at best, move us forward in the never-ending quest for good government. They give concrete examples of how to shake the pillars of the system and they should inspire all of us to reach for greater heights. We can take our government back from the oil companies and industry lobbyists and compel accountability and transparency again. There is always a new day dawning over America. Third parties show us the way and they make sure different voices are heard. This is critical for the health of our republic and we can use third parties to demand things like fiscal responsibility from the decision makers.

Chapter Seven: Foreign Policy

Understandably proud of this pre-eminence, we yet realize that America's leadership and prestige depend, not merely upon our unmatched material progress, riches and military strength, but on how we use our power in the interests of world peace and human betterment.[1]

~Dwight D. Eisenhower: 1961

Diplomacy or Empire?

The American Heritage Dictionary defines empire as:

1. A political unit having an extensive territory or comprising a number of territories or nations and ruled by a single supreme authority. 2. An extensive enterprise under a central authority: a publishing empire. 3. Imperial sovereignty, domination, or control.[2]

The central portion of the definition of empire is control. Writers comparing the modern day U.S. with an empire often neglect to consider the emergence of a multi-polar world. It is easy to understand if you think of the enormous change brought about by the fall of the Soviet Union. Prior to this, we fought proxy wars and built up weapons stockpiles in an uneasy "balance of terror"...and then there was one. How long can one military run it all? Or the more important question, do we really want to direct it all?

World history is filled with efforts by individuals to gain empire and motivate the public to follow a single leader into glory. Stalin and Mao were murderous, tyrannical thugs with a penchant for supremacy making Dick Nixon look like a saint. No respect is due Fidel Castro and Che Guevara or any others advocating bloodshed and tyranny. These despots breed fear and oppression which leads to further violence in an ever expanding circle. This is true whether it comes from the state or from criminals. After all, who is more oppressed; a society frightened by criminals, or one terrorized by its law enforcers?

The dream of America is to stand above these degraded forms of society. So many rulers demand allegiance to one individual instead of to a legal framework and they disdain diplomatic efforts. This is not what we want for our country!

Diplomacy has been held in contempt and yet it is crucial for building American influence, power, and decency. There is no question our government will falter if we continue to allow the leadership to pursue empire. Military might is important, there is no denying this, but it isn't the only way to deal with foreign affairs.

The tragedy of the attack on U.S. soil is it provided the hawks the chance to manipulate the national debate, a desire they salivated over since the Germans stormed the Berlin Wall. Some argue warlike aggression and bellicosity are keys to happiness and security. However, unrefined muscle breeds mistrust and it evolves into outright derision, lowering our global stature.

We can get beyond this by engaging in policies based in openness and by conducting trade which upholds human rights and environmental health. Imagine if it were a priority for American farmers to be paid a fair price for goods instead of shadow bureaucrats meeting clandestinely with tyrants and revolutionaries mediating seedy weapons deals.

Don't get me wrong, much of American foreign policy is a source of pride. The U.S. rushes to the aid of others. However, we also have an enormous arms industry aiding and abetting violent reactionaries around the globe. Then we act surprised at the terrible amount of existing conflict. We can do better.

Without the U.S. involvement rebuilding Western Europe and Japan after World War II the world would be in a very different position today. Who knows what the result would have been but the Soviets invaded Czechoslovakia and Hungary to smash dissent and if this was any indication, a great deal more conflict would have followed on the heels of World War II had the U.S. not gotten its hands dirty. Helping the world rebuild led to a more stable international order in the latter half of the twentieth century.

Despite President Bush's original assurances to the contrary, he began nation building with no shame. He failed to finish the job in Afghanistan when his approval ratings hovered somewhere around ninety per cent within the U.S. and very high around the world and stormed into Iraq, delivering shock and awe to the bemusement of the television audience. Years have gone by, war still rages, and all along there has been an odd series of shifting rationalizations from the White House regarding every decision regarding Iraq.

All Americans still pray for results, but since W landed on an aircraft carrier in a flight suit below a big sign saying it was over, people stopped believing in him. He has become as vile and pugnacious to the nation's citizenry as Lyndon Johnson or Richard Nixon. It is possible George Walker Bush will enter the history books as the most venal and ignorant creature in the national spotlight since 1974.

At the same time, W's supporters voice grave concern over the purple teletubby and the effect it may have on children's minds but have no difficulty seeing the President of the United States consistently speaking of killing with vivid fascination. Mighty Mouse was once accused by someone of snorting cocaine. He can snort all the cocaine he wants, as far as many in America are concerned, as long as he fights for justice.

The behind the scenes principals, however, are too busy coming up with downright weird analogies and conspiracy theories about these cartoon characters to notice America's plunge in world standing or the supposedly religious president grinning every time he talks about how many terrorists we have killed while steadfastly ignoring the plight of the innocent caught in the crossfire. It is ironic, yes, but this is the world in which vengeance takes precedence and empire is king.

The United States should never strive to become an empire. All the talk of rebuilding societies in our image and re-fashioning all international agreements to suit our purposes seems a bit like there is some sort of God complex governing the actions in the White House and we have been sucked into it. What a great and grand society we live in and how shameful it would be if we let it fall because a group of well funded cowards hijacked some planes and an indolent man led the soldiers into to a pre-determined war on the basis of some half-baked notions cooked up by a gang of rich geeks like Paul Wolfowitz, Richard Pearle, and Bill Crystal who believed it was W's destiny to march into history as some sort of modern Augustus.

The world watches and mainly waits for the departure of a man who may go down in history as more reviled than Richard Nixon and more demonized than Bill Clinton. The quest for empire was all well and good when word came from the people's house about mushroom clouds, secret meetings, and inevitable WMD. Like Orwell warned, at the time, we were told that Iraq was our enemy, it had always been our enemy and we had always fought Iraq. Things changed though, as they so often do with imperial ambitions.

We are told now that Iran is our enemy, it has always been our enemy, and we will be fighting Iran for the next fifty years. It is argued that they are insane and power hungry and they support terror. This despite the facts Iran has never ventured outside its own territory, it has a democratic government, of sorts, and Ronald Reagan sold weapons to them. World diplomacy can be messy and confusing to the untrained eye.

Radicals explain how those of us arguing for more diplomacy and less militarism are waving white flags—allowing Al Qaeda to win—we are, in this view, willing to surrender. This is just not true. I have yet to hear anyone explain what "winning" this war on terror means. It is an attempt to provide endless rhetoric to an insoluble problem while arming one faction against another and the result is infinite aggression.

Our way of life depends upon stronger moral behavior in foreign affairs. This is not surrender it is how we became a great nation. It is not cowardice but a call for vigor, honor, and upright conduct. It is essential to back those with alternative visions and not to allow "Big Brother" the ability to get in the door because…he will never leave.

Diplomacy is just the willingness to discuss world issues of trade and military conflict while standing firm with our founding principles. We have a tendency to be self-righteous when dealing with world affairs. This is understandable. Despite some assertions to the contrary, we have not actively pursued empire throughout our history. We have certainly expanded territory and even taken other cultures under our wing and some would call this a thirst for empire but all in all we have not expanded greatly or attempted to control all of international relations. We have to be careful because it is easy to fall into the trap built by being the most powerful country in a global age. The temptations are real and we must be wary of leaders who appeal to our worst fears.

The World Trade Center

It was remarked in the preceding paper that weakness and divisions at home would invite dangers from abroad; and that nothing would tend more to secure us from them than union, strength, and good government within ourselves.[3]

~John Jay: Federalist #5, 1788

No book discussing the United States of America in the twenty first century would be worth its weight without including the horror inflicted on September 11, 2001. Wherever the last plane was headed, it could not have been good. There is an old axiom stating "desperate times call for desperate measures." America woke up in desperation on that September morning. The attack was real and the purpose was clear...kill Americans...destroy our will. However, the terrorists discovered the consequences of attacking the United States. It can be assured the public will support any president following any act of terror on our land.

Terrorists beware, one more successful move on your part and many, many more will die in the heart of your lands. Voices of reason disappear quickly or they get drowned out by the war drums. Few citizens disagreed with going into Afghanistan. Many of us think the focus should have remained there and we believe Iraq was taken on for political and philosophical reasons and we believe it was wrong. This is not un-American, it is very American...standing against the tides for what we believe to be the truth.

Osama Bin Laden is a hero to many in the Muslim world for taking on the West with such audacity. He advances theories stating that the

U.S. is filled with greed and bloodlust and we are sustained by an unholy desire to turn the rest of the world into one giant colony.

He is wrong on so many levels. Bin Laden is no hero but history's biggest coward; an obscenely wealthy, spoiled child hiding in a cave or a palace, who knows. He believes wisdom correlates with aggression and takes distinct passages of the Koran out of the context of the whole to uphold his insane belief system. He proposes that all means justify the end of destroying Western Civilization, and the U.S. in particular. He will lose. Our debate needs to be over how our ideals will prevail over divisiveness and hostility.

It is offensive for politicians or pundits to state that those of us who disagree with their view wish to surrender and "wave a white flag."[4] It is untrue and unfounded...one more attempt to scare Americans into supporting one party and they should be ashamed. We must think more clearly about the ultimate consequences of our foreign policy in relation to terror. It is imperative we do not give in to our basest instincts for then we are falling into the terrorist trap. We need to uphold our ideals in the face of any and all dangers.

What rights do conspirators and terrorists have? The U.S. affords all people rights of trial by jury. It is at the center of the fight against tyranny. Against popular will, John Adams defended British soldiers who shot and killed colonists in the Boston Massacre in 1770. After World War II, many in Europe clamored for the immediate execution of Nazi war criminals. However, the Americans conducted the Nuremburg trials and exposed Nazi horrors for the entire world to see. Hopefully, in our time, terrorist trials will render a full accounting of the wicked, immoral mindset infecting these killers and once again supply lessons for all time. This is how we will win any war.

We should not shy away from debates over the reaction to terror. In the past, it was an unconscionable error turning against the troops in Vietnam. We all should honor the men and women defending the country. This, however, does not coincide with blind allegiance to policy makers. There are many who demand unwavering support for President Bush and every decision he has made. Many of these same individuals attacked President Clinton viciously while troops were in harms way in Somalia and in Kosovo. It appears they only desire unquestioning loyalty for one side.

We need to get beyond partisan nonsense relating to war and we need to always strive for peace. The Great Seal of the United States shows a bald eagle holding an olive branch with thirteen leaves in one talon and thirteen arrows in the other. Its head is turned toward the olive branch, symbolizing peace. It is an illustration of our desire for peace while we are ready to defend ourselves if we are forced to.

The disingenuous nature of the debate over war strategy is jaw dropping. These are important discussions over this so-called "war on terror." The United States, for good or ill, is the world's most powerful nation. Attacked and angered, we need to show the way by example and by exposing the crimes and murderous propensities of the gutless swine.

Curtailing civil rights and unlimited bloodshed eventually will force us down the dark path and this is when they win. When they are able to pervert our country and entice it into sliding down the scales of human injustice into their depths of depraved indifference and insolent disregard of the principles which made us great. We need to focus on taking the high road…which is never easy. We also have to consider the consequences of our retaliation without calling each other traitors, war criminals, war mongers, or other vile pseudonyms. Nazis and Communists are rare in our country. The wide range of possibilities open to us when we utilize diplomacy is astonishing but we have to move beyond our own limited vision.

Turning the Other Cheek

You have heard it said, "An eye for an eye and a tooth for a tooth." But I say to you, Do not resist one who is evil. But if any one strikes you on the right cheek, turn to him the other also.[5]

~Jesus of Nazareth, Matthew 5:39

But I say to you that hear, Love your enemies, do good to those who hate you, bless those who curse you, pray for those who abuse you.[6]

~Jesus of Nazareth, Luke 6:27

These are tough words to live by. Creative solutions hide in the shadows when rage and gloom obscure national dialogue and panic exacerbates the yearning for vengeance. Jesus remonstrated with his disciples about turning the other cheek. The message is to give ourselves up to others. We are, however, ultimately human and national pride swells in empathy with those murdered by mindless mercenaries.

Terrorists are weaklings preying on the innocent, capturing the minds of the poor and dispossessed and they do no Glory to God. It is easy to fill ignorant minds with revulsion and dread. Violence is the simple-minded, cruel, and foolish road and it leads to injustice. Martin Luther King Jr. did more for justice and fairness than Osama Bin Laden will ever even comprehend.

Suicide bombers and their sponsors choose a worldview existing behind the scenes. They know no humanity, only fear and repression. The fight on terror has become a war on the wicked. But these are immoral beings determined to gain as much influence as possible over the unfortunate in hopes of fomenting revolution. It would be a sad testimony to our awesome heritage if we were to continue taking the bait.

There is little likelihood of America turning the other cheek to any terrorist any more than we would ignore rapists and murderers. Nevertheless, it must be known these killers will be destroyed through not only strength but compassion and understanding for younger generations, for the real plight of the poverty stricken, and for those in need of jobs and education. We in America need to learn empathy for a population devoid of hope, watching as corporations dry up their wells and steal their resources without even-handed compensation. The expanding gap between the haves and the have-nots generates tension and violates basic human principles and it can lead to aggression.

While the connection between security and terror is real and the desire to use force is understandable, it is possible the methods are short sighted. In the end, they may reduce the nation from the heights of nobility to the depths of depravity. "Government of the people, by the people, for the people, shall not perish from this Earth,"[7] until the people are unable to uphold the foundations upon which the social order is constructed.

Holding the world hostage to our anxiety will not make us safer. Nothing can confirm convictions that order emerges from injustice, peace comes from war, or righteousness is derived out of mayhem. The most hateful individuals will always be out there. We have to figure out how to deal with them while upholding our own central philosophy.

America offers hope to oppressed people's around the globe. It promises a lasting place in the grand debate over social order to the least influential among us. We may feel beleaguered at times but we always return to our feet. For the first time in history, regular people have experienced the chance to affect national decisions. We can never give this up for any reason. Even the staunchest pacifist believes in taking a stand against what is cruel and wrong. Turning the other cheek is perhaps among the most courageous of acts. In the political sphere, the closest we can come is trying the best we can to avoid conflict through strength and diplomacy.

Peace is no longer very popular. Peace and Love are decried as foolish, idealistic dreams which can not stand up to hard, cold reality...but reality is not cold and hard. People are willing to help one another and live together. Peace and Love are unavailable to us only when we limit our abilities. The war on terror appeals to the weakest of emotions: hate, fear, and prejudice and it disguises itself in paeans: godliness, piety, righteousness, patriotism, and purity. Diplomacy should never be correlated to cowardice and empathy does not lack valor. We should never be afraid to search for strength, courage, and honor in the realization of our highest ideals.

The Declaration of Independence

When in the course of human events, it becomes necessary for one people to dissolve the political bands which have connected them with another, and to assume among the powers of the earth, the separate and equal station to which the Laws of Nature and of Nature's God entitle them, a decent respect to the opinions of mankind requires that they should declare the causes which impel them to the separation.[8]

~The Declaration of Independence

It has always been important for us to explain ourselves to the world. However, after 2001, we experienced trying times which trouble souls searching through the morass of human existence for meaning, for safety, and for purpose in a hostile world. Silly things took place like re-naming sliced potatoes in the capital and refusing to drink French wine to show others if they cross our purposes in any way, serious actions will be taken.

Hysteria bubbled up in 2002 and swept through the country for years. No action was too fierce, no rhetoric too harsh. Tavern goers advocated bombing the Middle East back to the Stone Age without the slightest hint of sarcasm. Meanwhile, an administration issued dire warnings to prop up the charade. So much for turning the other cheek!

In the most trying times, the signers of the Declaration of Independence chose to set down for posterity, and for the world at large, their reasoning. However, over the past years, any "decent respect for the opinions of mankind" quickly lost sway in our own frantic moments.

American citizens wondering over government actions were quickly shouted down, told to shut up, or called traitors. To President Bush's credit, when asked about protestors, he defended the practice as a right and tradition. At the same time, however, his administration worked tirelessly to adjust legal thinking to promote the authority of shadow agencies, open unabashed phone taps, and deny international agreements through word play and secret exploits. Along the way, we lost respect for others' opinions.

A nation at war always adjusts its rules of social engagement. John Adams supported the Alien and Sedition Acts. Abraham Lincoln suspended the right of habeas corpus, more sedition acts were passed during Woodrow Wilson's tenure in the White House, and people were jailed for speaking out against the war with Germany and Japan and then in Vietnam. Thinking comparatively, it is not surprising the Bush Administration expanded its influence over individual lives. News media tacitly supported each move the White House made and millions cheered as Rumsfeld's "shock and awe" reigned terror down on Baghdad; a fireworks show for a television generation. Unfortunately, it is possible that the war will never be over. It is the war on drugs with heavy firepower and the drivers are tireless unless they are forced to stop. There is too much money riding on the outcome and too much at stake for the largest of corporate America.

This is the danger of the war on terror. Tyranny can be ushered in to the cheers of an enthusiastic mob when horror makes the public shudder. This is not to say there are no threats to the United States. Timothy McVeigh and his fellow criminals were not Middle East terrorists, but it can be assumed if they were able to take the lives the nineteen terrorists did in 2001, they would have. Should the government then invade Michigan or Arizona because McVeigh hung his hat in those states? Belligerence has become our way to deal with the rest of the world and the end result is expanding antagonism escalating out of control.

The nation is at war. Of this there is little doubt. But who is it at war with? Iraq? Afghanistan? Iran? Islam? Terror? What of Sudan? How is the elimination of respect for life justified when it does not suit our self interest? The vague and self-centered ideal promoting greed as good can and should be challenged. Greed is a normal and necessary human emotion. It is part of, but it does not define humanity. A more intriguing view of life can open the world's beauty to people interested in seeing it.

War is no longer a last resort and leaders now seem to look forward to war instead of waiting and finding cracks in the armor of hate and anger. Impatience breeds contempt for serious consideration of diverse options. Unable to discuss issues, the country remains caught in the perils of combat.

Foreign policy is so sensitive now. It is a concern to even write or speak against the official policy because there are individuals in our country with such a limited view, they are poised waiting to attack all but loyalists to their cause. If we talk of: who knows how many civilian deaths, war profiteering, 4000 American military casualties, lack of the world's respect, forgotten Afghanistan, lost money, or an over-reliance on killing machines, we are accused of being partisan, anti-Bush, willing to surrender, or just plain traitorous. The self appointed thought police are lurking in the shadows pulling the strings on their puppets who hover menacingly over the airwaves waiting to enforce their new world order.

This is not the way to uphold the basic tenets of our nation. We can make our representatives follow our lead and we can show the way for the rest of the world if we think of our foundational philosophy. Our foreign policy needs to be more magnanimous and courageous than merely relying upon our array of weaponry and military might.

Chapter Eight: Morality

The Grand Old Party

Let us hope...that by the best cultivation of the physical world, beneath and around us; and the intellectual and moral world within us, we shall secure an individual, social, and political prosperity and happiness, whose course shall be onward and upward and which, while the earth endures, shall not pass away.[1]

~Abraham Lincoln, 1859

Honest Abe was talking to a group of farmers way back when as he spoke of the connections between the individual, society, and politics. As he so often did, he spoke in spiritual terms and he elevated the importance of morality. The Republican Party was founded in Wisconsin to combat the moral dilemma of the age, slavery. They worked to fight the possibility of slavery being admitted throughout the country through the expansion of the vile practice into new states. The party has a long and venerable tradition in relation to moral issues.

Today's foundations of their claim of the moral high ground emerge out of abortion and gay marriage. These are serious issues with ethical implications. Party leadership claims liberals require a litmus test for Supreme Court Justices, and argue they, of course, do not have any such test. As long as the nominee is a strict constructionist and is predisposed to granting a hearing to a case challenging Roe v. Wade and as long as he or she will assure the party faithful they will overturn Roe, then they can gain access to the highest court in the land. Seems like a litmus test doesn't it? If they are willing to rule against affirmative action and uphold any and all uses of police powers coming before the court, they can safely be called legal scholars. As long as they promise to provide no protection against the overpowering measures taken by the state, the right wing will call them great minds and they will be pleased.

The Grand Old Party lost what little grip they held on morality as they sunk deeper into their own depraved indifference. The American public decided in 2006 it was a morally bankrupt party, devoid of any interest in the strength and well being of the nation. It was perceived by many as if they sold their soul for absolute control and, despite claims of being a "big tent," citizens believed getting in required big money. The only thing keeping the party from following the fate of the Whigs (a party which dissolved in the mid-1800s) was the utter contempt the public has in their hearts for the Democratic Party. However, the great thing about democracy is that the parties can learn from past mistakes and re-emerge more responsive than before.

In 2000, "values voters" came out in force to show disdain for Bill Clinton's marital infidelity. Fifty percent of the voters believed George W. Bush wouldn't cheat on his wife, thus restoring "values" to the most powerful position in the nation and the birth of the "values voter." The story is longer and more complex but there is no need to go into it here. It appears at times that the "values voter" is a segment of our population working for government influence over private choices. Problems arise when certain segments of society believe their own values are more substantive and real than other views. It is then we lose appreciation for moral complexity.

Anyone taking part in the democratic process votes their values. Fiscal responsibility, privacy, tax reform, liberty, world peace, and economic stability are all values exhibited by voters every election cycle. Yet pollsters asked Republican voters in the 2004 election things like: "are values important to you" and so they think they established beyond any doubt the divide of between those voting for George W. Bush and those voting for John Kerry was based on morality. In their conviction, media and pollsters create segments of people based on their framing of issues. It is hard to be a fan of polls and pollsters, what insight they do give is dissected and parsed to justify pre-determined "analysis" and they affect trends as often as they predict them.

Among politicians, the moral high ground often comes from the platitudes shouted from the rooftops by those who feel no compunction about respecting other people's moral decisions and who have no problem shouting in self-righteous indignation. Going to church and believing in God don't matter anymore unless you proclaim your faith at the pulpit of popular media. Woe upon those who follow the words of James: "If any one thinks he is religious and does not bridle his tongue but deceives his heart, this man's religion is vain."[2] Yet anyone listening to these words in twenty-first century America likely will find herself out of office.

Every major candidate for the highest office of the land and the vast majority of contenders for lesser office, like the vast majority of the public, are Christian. It is time to move beyond the holier than thou phrases strategically placed in stump speeches for television or internet broadcasts. All it does is divide the nation and this doesn't offer solutions to our moral dilemmas. Moral authority does not necessarily emerge out of religious devotion.

Threats to Privacy

The right of the people to be secure in their persons, houses, papers, and effects, against unreasonable searches and seizures, shall not be violated, and no Warrants shall issue, but upon probable cause, supported by Oath or affirmation, and particularly describing the place to be searched, and the persons or things to be seized.[3]

~Fourth Amendment

Individual freedom requires privacy. Government spooks and corporate marketing sponsors will do anything to stomp it out of existence. However, today's spies pale in comparison to those of the past and this offers great optimism. Their efforts seem paltry when compared to the work of J. Edgar Hoover back in the fifties and sixties. Today, companies know who we call, credit card spending habits, and financial contributions. Anyone can go onto the internet and learn how much your house is worth. It is strange, this new world of open finances. But Hoover had it all. He knew what everyone in every office did. Law did not deter Edgar. He was not outside the law, he controlled the law. It is said Lyndon Johnson and Richard Nixon both salivated over Hoover's collection of dirty little secrets.

Here was a man who could tap a phone with no warrant and no oversight whatsoever. If ever a single person were able to bring down the central government and expose all the creepy lies and prove the truth of the innuendo, it was the head of the Federal Bureau of Investigation.

He started his career as a respectable, honorable G-man, hunting down the depraved, ruthless criminals holding the nation hostage with their ill gotten gain. But time and power caught up with him…it was too easy for him to get the goods on others.

No one asked him anything he didn't want to answer for so long, he learned to act with impunity. The fifties and sixties were the glory days for shady characters and back room deals worked out in fear of exposure. Hoover's files must have been massive. Most citizens can barely imagine the prestige which comes with secret tapes of everyone from the President to the lowliest state congressman. Hoover had raw power and a lifetime appointment as the chief law officer in the nation. He rubbed elbows with machine politicians and media moguls the likes of which we'll never see again such as Mayor Daly Sr. and William Randolph Hearst. These were the big guns and they make today's power brokers look like children.

The gig was up on past practices when Nixon played one too many hands. Nixon, despite current efforts to glorify the man, was a cheap and petty thug who exploited his elective office with little remorse until he got caught, looked around, and realized Edgar wasn't there to save him. These men believed privacy was O.K. for those who kept their mouths shut and their eyes open. They wanted people to spy on their neighbors. Edgar was not there to oversee the break-in at the Watergate Hotel and to fix the cover-up afterwards, he died in 1972. He would have never been so sloppy. And he would never have allowed Congress to legislate against him.

Hoover, like Johnson and Nixon, hated Bobby Kennedy with a passion bordering on madness. It is rumored during the last years of his life, he despised all things free and open and he had no time for justice. He traveled a long road through many travails of fighting the big dog criminals and even sending his agents south to take on the Klan but, in the end, the embittered decade of the sixties left him breathing with no soul, a warped ideologue looking to castigate his fellow citizens for their lack of purity and their desire to inquire about authority. His death left Nixon alone and confused and poor Dick would have been dragged out of the White House in chains if he hadn't moved out on his own.

So much discussion about the FISA laws requiring oversight of wiretapping and official intelligence gathering arose from the Patriot Act and we often forget where these laws came from. Anyone speaking their minds against the official propaganda in 1957 or 1967 was assured to be on Hoover's watch lists. Nixon was really only the bottom of the barrel. His was a tragedy of epic proportions. He was a man of fantastic abilities who worked hard for what he earned. He won by one of the biggest landslides in history against George McGovern in 1972 yet he was so paranoid leading up to the election anything was on the table. A third rate burglary begot a fourth rate presidency. And this, combined with Hoover's death, ushered in a period of intensive reform and oversight which we have with us to this day.

It is important to remember history. For those saying government does not do anything and it needs to get out of lives refuse to acknowledge the critical aspects of the FISA law. It came out of Johnson, Nixon, and Hoover's penchant for spying on Americans.

These things shed light on the current and future situations where the government deems it necessary to protect itself at the expense of the American citizen. Privacy will always be in peril. Today, the corporate world takes information and we give it away willingly every time we swipe a card. It is spooky to think what Hoover would know if he were alive today.

The ACLU is a monster in the eyes of many. Anything they do is outrageous and anti-American according to those who hate them. While it is easy to agree they take things too far at times, it is hard to deny the importance of an organization shaking up the government by protecting the rights of privacy requisite of a free nation.

There are those who will say if people have nothing to hide, let the government look. However, this is simply throwing in the towel and giving up on every ideal upon which our nation was created. The government will always need oversight. The press should provide it, and when they fail, the people have the ultimate authority over our elected representatives.

When privacy is ignored and governmental power assumes complete dominance over domestic actions, we face grave dangers. Citizen vigilance is a cornerstone of liberty, which walks hand in hand with security. A secure nation is a free nation and freedom requires the right to govern ourselves and to rule over our own affairs. We, as individuals, have the capability to make moral decisions without government oversight.

Who Governs Our Lives?

Nothing is more certain than the indispensable necessity of government; and it is equally undeniable that whenever and however it is instituted, the people must cede to it some of their natural rights, in order to vest it with requisite powers.[4]

~John Jay, Federalist #2, 1788

Governing versus freedom straddles a tenuous line. Social Security, according to many great minds, is heading down a dark and empty path filled with the horror of empty coffers and poverty stricken seniors while an entire population loses its ability to pay for anything but minimum payments due on the national debt. Reform is essential. Nearly everyone agrees on this. The question here is whether it is appropriate for the government to involve itself in what is essentially a private issue...retirement.

Social Security is not government intrusion but a safety net for the general welfare which needs to be protected. It is a moral question for the future. So many young people have been convinced the program is going away they are willing to give it up and I believe they will rue the day this eventually happens. This is a simple program which is so beneficial to the majority of Americans I find it hard to believe anyone wants to destroy it.

President Bush pushed Social Security onto the national agenda in 2005. For this, he should be commended. However, he didn't provide any substantive proposal to adjust the system. He assured the American people that all ideas were "on the table." However, he failed to provide any guidance and seemed to believe just saying he wanted something done would make things happen.

It was rumored Bush learned from Clinton's complete failure to reform health care. The Clinton administration offered specific proposals and the anti-health care reform powers organized like they never had before. So the Bush administration, according to this theory, brought the issue of Social Security to the national discussion but refused to offer concrete ideas, just vague notions of private accounts. He made restructuring Social Security a major platform of his presidency and, like Clinton before him, he failed. Our system stands against this sort of single minded transformation. What we need is to get a panel of intelligent, thoughtful folks who can craft a plan for re-organization. Ronald Reagan and Tip O'Neil accomplished this very thing in the 1980s.

Social Security is the most popular and, it can be argued, useful federal program ever enacted and opponents came out of the woodwork to attack Bush's plans to get government out of the retirement game. Despite the importance of the issue and what appeared to be good intentions, he failed to bring people from all sides of the issue together. Leaders need to have at least some semblance of humility and realize just saying something must be done won't make it so. Reform takes work. It is easy to commend Bush for raising a critical topic but Social Security destruction has been on his party's agenda for thirty years so he really didn't do anything requiring much political courage.

Nothing activates the political sphere more emphatically than issues surrounding Social Security. Bush pushed for reform of the program but got nowhere by taking an ideological instead of a pragmatic stance. Back in the 1980's, Reagan created a bi-partisan commission to examine fiscal restraints and extend the program's viability. Unfortunately, Bush was unable, or unwilling, to work effectively with anyone who saw things differently than he did. He threw the program out there, spoke about his scheme regarding privatization, and left it to his own party in Congress to take the bullet when it failed.

It is a recurring theme within Bush's presidency. There is a failure of leadership and an insistence that all public policy conform to a narrow view or nothing at all. Millions of elderly citizens are allowed to spend the twilight of their years in relative independence and financial stability thanks to the Social Security system—nobody gets rich on it.

The coming election will see politicians, pundits, and experts coming out of the woodwork claiming they know how to fix it but if the plans include privatization and leaving old folks to fend for themselves, it will end in disaster. One of the dilemmas we confront...we can have the best plan in the world and without an understanding of politics, working with others, negotiation, and compromise, nothing will get accomplished. This is true no matter which party is in control.

The nation consistently needs leadership that is not afraid to work with everyone from the beginning to craft long term solutions benefiting current and future generations and keeping this program intact. Enacted after the devastation of the Great Depression, Social Security has lasted over seventy years and saved millions from a retirement of desperation. The choices are hard and the White House skirted the issue while making it seem like a priority.

It is essential that we remember: when the President traveled around hyping people up on his proposals, the House and the Senate were in solid control of the Republican Party. Still, no one wanted to hear W's ideas about private accounts. No wonder it went nowhere.

Too many regular folks depend on monthly checks to risk moving all that money into a private system reliant on the whims of the stock market. You don't have to go back to the 1930's to see devastating effects a stock market downturn can have on real lives. The idea of raising the level of taxation has been offered as a solution by a number of candidates. Raising the retirement age would work but there should be a chance for those working in jobs which take a toll on the body would be able retire early.

The idea of a higher income level for taxation and incentives for IRAs and 401Ks is a good one but we need to make sure no real people slip through the cracks. Elected leaders should be willing to take a hard look at these sorts of issues and to do what is necessary including… gasp...compromise with others. Or else, like New Orleans, by the time any action is taken, the frog will already be boiled. The lessons here include: government can be good but things need to be reconsidered through time, and those working on issues will never accomplish anything with a "take no prisoners" attitude and rhetoric.

All of the responses surrounding the coming Social Security crises can be brought together under a realistic plan to save the system. It is too important to the health and safety of our country in this century. We should not shy away from the problem, but we should not over-estimate the dangers either. There are ways to fix it but until regular people take the initiative to guide the policy-makers, Social Security will sit in limbo. It is one of the greatest moral quandaries facing us today.

And then there's Medicaid.

Federal Budget

The Congress shall have the power to lay and collect taxes, duties, imposts and excises, to pay the debts and provide for the common defense and general welfare of the United States.[5]

~Article 1, section 8, U.S. Constitution

Fiscal priorities show our moral decisions and they demonstrate our national priorities. Unfortunately for those demanding smaller government, people don't seem to want it. They want Social Security, Medicare, Medicaid, and inter-state highways. They look to the federal government to help the least fortunate and to protect folks from market whims. They also desire oversight of the corporate world which has repeatedly shown its failures to patrol its own waters. Plus, voters repeatedly hire candidates who bring the goods back from the federal government. It is common for the most virulent anti-tax, anti-federal individuals to gain influence over government spending priorities. This generates strife when the party in power adamantly argues for small government and the end result is a fascination with ignoring moral choices while they use appointments to advance ambitions and pay back supporters.

The most famous of these situations arose with FEMA director Michael Brown aka: Brownie. To the astonishment of a captivated nation watching as the city of New Orleans fell apart at the seams, the President praised this man who had no emergency management knowledge or training for a debacle which would prove to be a main cause of the downward slide of his presidency. Like the "Mission Accomplished" sign, Katrina showed the public how far out of touch with reality the president and his cabinet was.

The same thing happened to his father when Bush I failed to take Hurricane Andrew seriously and, just before his re-election bid in 1992, voters perceived a callousness which helped cost him the bid to stay in the White House.

George Herbert Walker Bush was a war hero and a pragmatist. Barbara Bush exhibited all the best qualities of a first lady. However, like Jimmy Carter, George I was a poor manager and a miserable communicator whose party felt betrayed and whose countrymen and women lacked the trust requisite to give him the nod a second time.

Hurricane Andrew caused the first president Bush a great deal of heartache and bad press for much the same reason his son was castigated for failing in 2005. FEMA is one of those agencies conservatives despise. It involves itself in local matters and they think that if you live in a hurricane zone, a flood plain, or a fire hazard area, you should take care of yourself and assume responsibility for your choices and just deal with it.

So, FEMA takes a back seat to other priorities like bomb building and space weaponry in Republican administrations. However, disaster relief is important and it affects real people. For good or ill, disaster victims have come to expect federal support in response to natural disasters. Once leaders take actions to eliminate or politicize what they consider to be systemic evils such as FEMA, they should expect an outcry when calamities arise. Effective planning, preparation, and training cost less and help more than working to destroy a federal agency.

Forest fires, for example, use vast amounts of resources each and every year as firefighters risk their lives to battle blazes and save people and homes. However, forest restoration, including prescribed burns and thinning, renews forest health and reduces the danger of wildfire. Those who reduce the flammable material on their own property and fire retardant building materials are safer in the event of wildfire. Increasing homeowners move into forested areas susceptible to wildfires without comprehending the risks. If the federal government helps in the first place, it is much less expensive for all of us.

The same can be said with health care and education. Pre-natal care and teaching children early saves society remarkable amounts of money over the long term. Small initial investments can generate tremendous social profit. The days of the country doctor are long gone and modern medicine is expensive. We need to figure out a way to assure medical care for those who don't have it or can't afford it. Uninsured costs affect all of us for those costs are absorbed and paid for somewhere. These are true moral issues we need to consider as we prepare for the world of tomorrow.

Chapter Nine: Religion

We pray that peoples of all faiths, all races, all nations, may have their great human needs satisfied; that those now denied opportunity shall come to enjoy it to the full;
that all who yearn for freedom may experience its spiritual blessings;
that those who have freedom will understand, also, its heavy responsibilities;
that all who are insensitive to the needs of others will learn charity;
that the scourges of poverty, disease and ignorance
will be made to disappear from the earth, and
that, in the goodness of time, all peoples will come to live together
in a peace guaranteed by the binding force of mutual respect and love.[1]
~Dwight D. Eisenhower, 1961

What About God?

Ike left the Oval Office with a prayer for the human spirit and a hopeful message for mankind among other things. He was a warrior and lifelong servant who spoke of God's blessing on America in his farewell to the nation. All presidents have been Christian. They have proclaimed, at times their piety and at others their humility in the presence of the Almighty. Ike's words remind us this does not mean we disregard the devotion of others but we should pray for all humankind, as Jesus would. He was a smart man, Ike. His parting address is filled with pearls of wisdom, heartfelt concern for the country, and a bit of advice on how to keep us strong, safe, and free.

Strength, safety, and freedom were not three distinct aspects of American life in Ike's mind but entwined together forming the fabric of the national quilt. Once one starts to unravel, the rest go along till there's just a pile of yarn, without the complexity of the pattern which had taken so long to knit together. God has a special place in public life. Our creator provides the rights and liberties enshrined in our Constitution. Three quarters of this country practices Christian religion and it is good. Something has been happening over the past few decades, though, and it is disturbing and irrelevant to good governance.

Our nation's laws are founded in the Judeo-Christian tradition but judges need to have a strong, liberal education, and a full knowledge of American Constitutional law. They also need a bit of common sense and understanding. We are a nation of laws but compassion is also important to us. It is a touchy subject and no one is happy with any effort to speak of religion and politics.

God has turned into a blunt instrument with which to bludgeon political opponents. This is a far cry from the Lord Lincoln prayed to for wisdom. Religious discussion has descended to the realm of antagonism, without the realization we are all God's children and without acknowledging that our people strive every day to do what is good and honest and true. In the pursuit of freedom and justice respect for other religious beliefs is vital and we need to stop politicizing religion. Leave the judgments to God.

Legacies

Where there is no guidance, a people falls; but in an abundance of counselors there is safety

~Proverbs, 11:14[2]

There are two men walking down the gang plank into history shrouded by failure and drowned in a sea of antagonism. Jimmy Carter, the 39th president, was honest to a fault and unable to unify even his own party, let alone the country. Few people liked Carter as president. Ted Kennedy opposed him for the nomination of the Democratic Party in 1980 and no one wanted him in office by the time Reagan trounced him in the general election. Carter joined the ranks of such illustrious one term presidents as Herbert Hoover and William Howard Taft. Gerald Ford was never elected to any national office and Lyndon Johnson voluntarily departed in shame but Carter, George Bush I, Hoover, and Taft lost their bids for re-election.[3] To his credit, Carter has worked tirelessly since he left office to make the world a better place and he has reduced the negative impressions he garnered from his presidential term.

George W. Bush lost the popular vote in 2000, a dubious honor he shares with Benjamin Harrison and Rutherford B. Hayes. Harrison won the 1888 election against sitting Democratic President Grover Cleveland by 65 electoral votes while earning 98,000 less popular votes. In 1876 Hayes lost to Democrat Samuel Tilden by 250,000 and won the electoral count by 1, a special commission was enacted to decide between the two based on a tie. Bush won a second term by the lowest margin of a sitting president since Harry Truman but even Harry won the Electoral College by 114. W took away his re-election with 35 and claimed it as a mandate. You have to return to the re-election of Woodrow Wilson in 1916 to find a sitting president with a narrower electoral margin—Wilson won by 22.[4]

Carter and Bush are polar opposites of just about everything except both proclaim faith to be the dominant facet of their lives. Neither will likely go down in history as a positive leader or a revered figure by the end of their terms in office. Jimmy has already proved this and George has received such sustained low approval ratings it is hard to see how scholars could dig him out of the mess he created for any sort of encouraging legacy.

On the other hand, Harry Truman was not well liked when he left office and historians examined his life a bit differently. There are also think tanks determined to revise history and restore Richard Nixon's positive image for future generations. From the lens of the future, who knows what they will say of W. The point really is just this: religion is not owned by any ideology. We desperately need to learn basic respect for the right of religious diversity which helped the founders create a framework based in freedom.

The Bill of Rights includes a religious clause because of history and the overwhelming evidence of violence and cruelty arising out of connections between spiritual and political authority. The proof is widespread…The Crusades, Britain's religious wars, the Spanish Inquisition, and the Salem witch trials.

Religion or spirituality plays a major role in the lives of most individuals in one form or another. There is no need to use its influence to enforce one agenda. Bush and Carter illustrate the importance of faith to leaders of a wide range of philosophies, they are not meant to point out some failure of religious presidents. Clinton was a lifetime Baptist and Reagan built his presidency around the Christian Coalition and I would call both of their presidencies exceptional examples of productive periods in American politics.

It is disingenuous to argue religion plays no role in political life. For all the carping about Jefferson's anti-religious views, it is obvious the founding fathers held strong beliefs in something beyond our material world. For the majority of them faith came from Christianity. The founding fathers were the brightest of their time, they understood the past and they knew the perils of uniting religious and secular control. It is futile to argue about the abolition of faith in public life. It will not happen. We now have to figure out how to ask the questions God would ask of us.

Does God want government to ignore the plight of the working poor? Does God appreciate greed as a driving philosophy? Should we continue to act carelessly toward the Earth? Why didn't Jesus take up Satan's offer to rule the cities when he was confronted in the desert? He refused power and riches because they meant nothing to him. Somehow, from this, some have reached the conclusion that only those striving for riches and determined to advance personal influence are worthy of the Lord. It might be good to remember that the Lord warned of wolves in sheep's clothing and not of sheep in sheep's clothing.

Presidential faith is pretty standard fare in a country of deep religious convictions but recently, proud and boastful proclamations of church and piety have assumed critical roles within party politics. This is the danger of combining religion and politics. It is one more thin line in our reality.

Religion has a place in politics. The founders reached into the well of divinity to uphold the principles of liberty. Abolitionists used devotion to argue against slavery. Faith played a part in arguing for worker's rights, child labor laws, women's rights, and it was important in the conservation movement. Dr. Martin Luther King Jr. rallied the faithful from all persuasions to pressure the powerful and force civil rights legislation.

The "wall of separation" between church and state does not mean faith will not guide individual choices. It means no one party and no one group of believers have special privileges under our Constitution.

Those folks denigrating worship and producing evidence of the founding fathers' atheism are simply wrong. There is really no other way to put it. On the other hand, so are the factions considering every founding father a staunch advocate of state sponsored religion. Truth and reality here, like so many other things—history, politics, biblical scholarship, is more convoluted, complex, and diverse than many would like it to be. Raising armies of Holy warriors in the name of one particular ideology demeans the essence of America. We need to respect one another no matter what our relationship is with whatever we conceive God to be and we need to get over the religious divide.

Otherwise, like the Trojan horse, efforts to produce a society divided by divine caveat will seep into the statehouse and bring with it death and ruin in an unrelenting quest for religious purity. This is not what we want as a nation. Religious principles offer guides but we need to start honoring each other's beliefs. I think God can handle it.

The State and God

Render therefore to Caesar the things that are Caesar's, and to God, the things that are God's.[5]

~Jesus of Nazareth, Matthew 22:21

Among the earliest exclamations of the separation of church and state comes from the savior himself. Coins had Caesar's likeness on them at the time Jesus walked among humanity and he admonished his followers to keep separate the meaning of the two. Caesar held sway over the political world which was, according to Jesus, different and inferior to the precepts of God. Nevertheless, building the pulpit in the public square is not a new phenomenon. Lately, however, God has been dragged into the muck and mire and He invariably supports one particular worldview.

Neither side can stake a claim to the will of the Almighty. It is offensive when public employees justify every action and idea as if it was majestically confirmed from above and the Constitution warns of this sort of deception. We all need a little more humility about the Creator. We could all work on consistently improving our own lives and building a stronger world whether we have faith, we don't believe, or whatever form our faith takes. It is possible we are sometimes wrong about God. Only She knows.

No one, at least no one with any sanity, would call for a president to denounce religion or to take up Buddhism in the oval office. Whatever your predilections regarding White House activities and the meaning of God in the twenty-first century, it is for the unassuming and the meek to worry about jokes regarding religion. Yes, it can be taken seriously but it should not be such a weighty issue.

It might be good if we pondered the joy of God a bit more often. Laughter and beauty are one with the Creator. Our failures just show that none of us are perfect but we must still strive for greatness. Our worldly achievements do not last for very long but our country has a strong and flexible history and we can deal with each other on a higher level. We don't need to follow the path of so many around the world who are lost in age old religious conflicts which seem to have no end. We have a long way to go but respect is not so hard. It seems God probably knows this and understands that, after all, we are only human.

The First Amendment

Congress shall make no law respecting the establishment of religion or prohibiting the free exercise thereof.[6]

~First Amendment

The First Amendment is clear. It protects the right of religious worship and maintains an assurance against the establishment of state sponsored religion. Many people in the modern world take the extremes of these two views and argue that one or the other completely dominates for all time due to the founders' views. On the one hand, some find any mention of God or Jesus as insulting and offensive to their views, on the other hand, many believe God has been taken out of the public square against majority will. In the latter view, we have evolved into a nation of godless heathens. In the former, any religion is too heavy handed. It is not a simple subject. It evokes heart-felt, passionate emotions on both sides.

A widespread condemnation sweeps over the country after every disaster or difficulty. Certain folks argue we are a godless nation, not unlike the Soviet Union of old. This is why New York was attacked, why crime runs rampant, it is the genesis, so to speak, of Hurricane Katrina, and it is the cause behind every school shooting. There is only one serious flaw with this assertion....Americans are overwhelmingly Christian. And when we add in other religious affiliations, we find atheists form an exceedingly small percentage of the population. Certain religious purists need to lighten up.

There has been a gigantic row over the pledge of allegiance and whether or not we should say "under God." I would be curious to know how many citizens know that God wasn't in the pledge until the communist scares of the 1950s. It seems if a parent does not want their child to say it, fine. That is what freedom is.

Freedom is not only for those who believe as the majority does. If this is what freedom is, then it is meaningless. As for being Godless...racism is lower than ever, the fascists in white hoods are on the run, Indians are no longer beaten for speaking their native tongues, children don't work in mines, the environment is cleaner, and large numbers of young students enter the Peace Corps, the ministry, teaching, nursing, and law. We will always have to get better, that is a part of life in a democracy but we are moving in a positive direction and we should never forget this. I'm proud of today's America.

Putting God into schools is a touchy subject. It can be viewed as state sponsored religion and an attempt to control developing minds. Others believe strongly in the edifying effects of religious organizational structure and the moral persuasion allowing religion into the classroom would bring. Who, then, gets left out? The Jew, the Muslim, the Buddhist? Christianity is not dead and keeping the Lord out of the public school system does not bring Him....or Her....any closer to destruction. The conception of God promoted by judgmental, indignant, ideologically driven, modern day purists is so small.

Atheists and agnostics angered by every theological reference wishing to never hear of the Lord or the ways Judeo-Christian values shaped the country exhibit the same immature antagonism and panic revealed by the holy rollers. There is nothing wrong with public mangers, ten commandment stones, or saying Merry Christmas. Essentially, everyone needs to chill a bit and learn a little bit of respect for one another. We will never all agree and attempts to enforce this type of uniformity create a path to repression. We need to be satisfied with our diversity.

Renounce God or rejoice in Her...it is very personal, a choice protected by the Constitution. God might be a little sad about our inability to worship together as a nation but She's probably more irritated by all the traipsing around and self congratulations of those who judge others on the pulpit of public opinion. We have to be careful here. There is always a tendency to look backwards and to long for the simpler days of old. However, the old days were not that great in many ways...white folks could own other people, men beat their wives, and children were just chattel to be sent out for a day's wages. Women could not vote, Indians couldn't practice their religions or speak their native languages, the poor had no recourse to justice. You get the picture. Not everything in our past is glorious and worthy of praise. This does not mean there was not a lot of good but we do have our scars to bear. If God was with the nation then, it seems safe to assume He still is.

If faith requires belief that God is the cause for unnecessary hardship resulting from natural disasters as if the United States is a modern Sodom…Godless and impure, instead of holding the cretins responsible, from local and state officials straight to the White House and Congress for not taking heed of widespread warnings and to the leaders of the wealthiest nation in history for not even trying to deal with issues of poverty, injustice, and the environment, and failing to consider the effects of a business at all costs mentality, then we will only get what we deserve.

There are people who blame all human problems on lack of faith. They insist terrorist attacks are caused by heathens and God, while sad, is merely getting out of the way like the people of this country have asked "Him" to. According the 2000 census, over 75% of the country still identifies as Christian. The Godlessness proclaimed by self-appointed modern Pharisees simply does not exist. Granted 25% of the population describing their beliefs as not Christian in one way or another is much higher than it used to be but there's a host of other religions represented in our society as well.[7] Maybe, if there were a bit less judgment and a little more compassion, fewer people would be turned off by the fanatics.

It is the sort of vile garbage which is infuriating about the zealots. They demand certain things: stick God back in the schools and there will be no more murder, mayhem, or terrorism; ban abortions because that is God's will; force the Jew kid to say a prayer to Jesus; stick the Muslim in Bible study; then, and only then, will the rest of the culture be safe. God, in the arguments of too many tele-preachers, pays more attention to the super bowl than he does to our political world and some of the human disasters caused by our own neglect. A little more respect, a touch of love, and a bit less of the angry, wrathful old man upstairs might make a world of difference. We have freedom to choose our earthly fates.

Hurricane Katrina was the result of failures at every level. It was created through numerous administrations, both Democratic and Republican. It seems unlikely God, at least the Christian Lord and the

Savior Jesus Christ, would ever turn their back to anyone. Where do these notions come from? Would God really turn away in despair? Do they think God can't figure out human frailty and emotion? Or that He doesn't comprehend political battles?

When did the wondrous Eden exist in America? It is not today, and never will be, an atheistic nation. The Soviets tried to smite God. God waited them out. It was easy…only seventy years. There are churches and synagogues and mosques that adorn the land of the free and religion, the practicing of one's love of God, is one of the most significant aspects in the lives of hundreds of millions around the country. As for atheists…so what if some folks don't believe. How does this cripple or corrupt society? It doesn't.

American history crams into its narrative volumes of hate, crime, and cruelty born in ignorance and fear. The perception that modern folks are living in Hell highlights the belief that things were better long, long ago, in a distant land where smells were sweet and thrift and industry ruled the land. The hearty individual made a name for himself way back when, in the days of whiskey and tobacco. Back when a lynching and a burnt cross was just a bit of rabble rousing on a Saturday night, blowing off steam on a hot Louisiana night or when scalping an injun was just part of the game.

There are a lot of things wrong in America: a lost generation roams inner cities living in penury and hopelessness; kids shoot each other; millions have no health insurance; the environment is in peril; education for the young and care for the elderly need to be better; there is a lack of respect for authority and a general attitude of get what you can while you can….Hollywood style; the well off and educated are taught to watch out only for their own and to ignore the plight of others; greed permeates and the super rich have bizarre desires to get onto Forbe's 500 instead of the cover of Philanthropy Today. Still, we will get past all this with honest talk and hard work.

Through it all the U.S.A. has not merely survived, but thrived and created ingenious benefits to humanity. Today's issues are not insoluble—daunting—scary at times—but we will never give up on our dreams. It takes effort to overcome the thornier predicaments of a society more complex and intricate than any history has seen. But what the United States has is so much larger and grander than anything that can be taken away from it. Using God as a political weapon demeans our spirit and trounces freedom. The founders warned us about this.

Places of worship are as strong today, if not stronger, than they have ever been. There may be a portion of society that stands outside of that arena, but it just doesn't make sense that God would turn away because He is not in schools. Or that He sadly watches as the poorest and weakest drown in tidal pools of despair.

No, if God is sad, it seems likely that He is for different reasons...those at the top of the economic ladder seem to care little for their fellow man; tax relief and business at all costs are the overriding orders of the day; it is too costly to figure out a way to keep the wetlands She created to absorb hurricane winds; strip malls are more important than nesting areas; education means shuffling kids between kindergarten and jail instead of teaching the lessons of history and civics; prisons evolved into a source of revenue and are no longer something to be ashamed of but they provide jobs; cheap stuff, and lots of it, is more dear than intricate weavings telling stories about humanity; and since discussions of money replaced talks of justice and righteousness long ago.

People who live through tragedy don't need the self-righteous pointing tainted fingers. I do not believe God is not so small-minded as to turn His or Her proverbial back on people, especially since the vast majority has not turned their backs on God. The petty feel obliged at every turn to make sacrifice at the altar of public opinion. Through knowledge, work, and, yes, faith, the system of government will allow us to solve any problem, overcome all adversity, and win every challenge. We don't need religious tests to assure the nobility of our intentions.

It is hard to know how many people of faith live decimated by Katrina, and who knows how many others will feel the wrath of future natural disasters. It is a safe bet an awful lot of those folks prayed before the storm, during the storm, and after the storm. God grants these people the spirit to sustain and rebuild their lives, politics should provide the tools for them to do so.

Chapter Ten: The Environment

Will We Crash and Burn?

The conservation of our natural resources and their proper use constitute the fundamental problem which underlies almost every other problem of our national life.[1]

~Theodore Roosevelt, 1907

Throughout our history, environmental actions have been prominent in public debates. Native Americans hold the planet in high regard and they have shared their knowledge with us in many ways. The earliest of forebears came to this land because it was open and free. Nature is a cornerstone of liberty and the land underfoot defines who we are.

Nature strengthens individuals and expands minds. Hiking, biking, backpacking, Four-wheeling, hunting, fishing, and picking natural herbs are all part of the American experience. Lands such as the Grand Canyon, Yellowstone, the Smoky Mountains, the Everglades, the Great Lakes, free flowing wild and scenic rivers, and more offers arenas for wildlife and humans to come together. They are not only resources but national treasures without which, we would be much poorer. America's health and beauty requires continuous protection. The conservation ethic is strong and need not be compromised for short term gain. This is a lesson we must constantly be aware of if we are to protect our heritage now and for tomorrow.

Contentious environmental issues break open political rhetoric into all out war. Yet there are so many areas that citizens can agree when they push past those initial feelings of distrust. The fight between economics and environmental health is hard to overstate. Yet traveling to cities it becomes difficult to understand how people do not see the degradation of nature unfolding before their eyes: traffic congestion, smog, sprawl, the loss of land to endless development; water pollution, toxins in the soil, garbage piling up or floating on barges, concrete winding its way throughout cities in ways that make attempts to bike or walk untenable.

There is a great deal of hope these days though and we need more efforts aimed at healing the rift between humans and nature. Standing on the Acropolis in Athens nearly twenty years ago, it felt as if I were witnessing both the beginning and the end of Western Civilization. It is an amazing feeling to be there, where thoughtful and engaged men planted the seeds of democracy. At the same time, out over the city, the smog was thick as molasses. Tourists, far more worldly and wealthy than I, lamented within earshot of the shame of it all.

Now, cities and businesses are taking steps toward green building. Rooftop gardens in metropolitan areas cool the heat in the summer and help (even if just a little) combat the smog. Areas of land that have been devoid of the trees that stabilize the soil and hold water that would otherwise flood are being re-forested. Wangari Maathai plants trees in an effort to provide sustenance and self reliance for local women throughout Africa. She started small but she understood the connection between humanity and a healthy ecosystem and she teaches what she knows through perseverance and fortitude. We can learn from Ms. Maathai. Within the realm of our politics…concerned citizens can move the course of humanity.

Hope Springs Eternal

Climb the mountains and get their good tidings. Nature's peace will flow into you as sunshine flows into trees. The winds will blow their own freshness into you, and the storms their energy, while cares will drop off like autumn leaves.[2]

~John Muir

The destruction of the oil industry, or any other industry, will not create safe environments, nor do any thinking people truly advocate decimating industry or profit motives. However, companies do need to be held accountable for repairing damaged lands, restoring roadless areas, and acting as responsible stewards of the Earth in their charge. Many companies are taking steps in the direction of environmentally friendly production and distribution but this is also the birth of green-washing; making use of symbolic gestures to gain public support in lieu of substantive proposals. We need to be aware of this possibility which is open to mammoth multi-national corporations.

Technological solutions offer themselves increasingly for the benefit of man and nature. However, too often, suited, perfumed goons marching government hallways effectively squash efforts to modify the power structure and to re-think social goals. Then we lose hope. Standing up to trained guerillas supporting the dominant party at all costs is scary. At the same time, lobbyists spend their lives influencing policy and advancing their own agendas, often at public expense.

People care about environmental health and we are gaining more understanding about how to affect institutions and policy prescriptions aimed at preserving the best of our nation. Both parties have long histories of environmental strategies. This allows them to take on the issues relating to environmental health. However, they will only do so if we prod them and we demand action.

Industry is critical to this process. Business executives have to move their companies forward or, inevitably, there will be regulation once people have simply had enough of pollution and disregard for the natural aesthetic. It costs money to protect and preserve natural resources and nature as a whole and it seems fair to have the federal government involved in these efforts.

Take Superfund, the legislation mandating cleanup of the most toxic sites in the country. Every citizen in the United States has benefited from industrialization. Transportation and goods provide choice to the consumer and the free flow of material possessions heralded a new age. There is no reason why the country should not take steps to clean up the vestiges of past excess, conducted with vague knowledge of industrial consequences. Restoration is possible in all sorts of arenas, old mines, contaminated dump sites, the elimination of old roads, tree planting, de-commissioning aging dams, and renovating wild, scenic rivers, to name just a few.

Industrial activity was never confined to small remote areas. The effluent dumped into the Cuyahoga River helped businesses manufacture goods shipped to every corner of the country. The wholesale destruction of Western old growth forests provided timber to the Midwest and East Coast. Somewhere along the line, someone has to pay for cleaning expenses. It seems right and responsible for all of us to pitch in and we do that through our federal tax dollars.

Keeping the federal government out of environmental protection leads to less expensive, filthier practices of production and it removes incentives to clean up existing areas. We can do better. Leaving environmental health solely in the hands of the market allows corporate interests to ignore the real costs of their actions and leave problems to be dealt with somewhere down the road, with unspecified entities paying the costs and absorbing the risks and that's downright foolish.

Kyoto and Bali

Energy security and climate change are two of the great challenges of our time. The United States takes these challenges seriously. The world's response will help shape the future of the global economy and the condition of our environment for future generations.

~President George W. Bush, 2007[3]

The United Nations Climate Change Conference in Bali, Indonesia meandered through without coming up with much of anything. After ten years of the Kyoto Protocol, disparate nations like Canada and Russia did not reach target reductions of CO2 while Europe held fast to its self-proclaimed superiority in Earth friendly social actions.

The United States, for its part, dismissed any concerns and disregarded the debate carried on by the rest of the world by assuring all involved it would come up with its own climate program by the middle of 2008. Apparently, The Bush administration had not had the opportunity to ponder the issue since W crossed the threshold on Pennsylvania Ave in January, 2001. In their infinite wisdom, this administration took the stance that nobody else in the world should try to take actions to protect the planet. So why waste their time?

No matter what the administration had in mind, (likely the desire to put off any sort of action until George is happily clearing brush and Dick is doing whatever maniacal control freaks with a penchant for frightening people do with spare time in Wyoming), its response to the calls of the world show it to be the ignorant step-child of the past. In our past, the United States defeated Communism, Nazism, and Fascism, and gave humanity the Nuremburg trials, the United Nations, and the Geneva Convention. It is too bad if we continue to ignore our legacy.

George W. Bush took on the big issues, as long as they didn't affect his dated ideas relating to business. Dangerous propositions abounded in Bali, creating panic and terror in the confined world that was the Administration. They seemed to believe industry is conducted the way it has always been done. No moving forward. No using American know how and pragmatic sensibilities to face and fix any problem.

For years now, Uncle Sam has seemed like an ignorant, blind fool wandering through the forest as if his eyes were poked with sharp sticks depriving him of sight while blood dripped down his cheeks, inducing incomprehensible horror and unwarrantable insanity. This administration reminds people of a straight jacketed extra in the filming of the Night of the Living Dead, who missed the bus and wandered helplessly around the graveyard, taunted by winos while rabid dogs nipped at his heels. Even circus clowns avoid such demon like apparitions.

Unfortunately for the administration, the country, and the world, no matter how right the White House inhabitants have been about anything, the way they conduct themselves is just creepy to the rest of the world and to at least ½ of the patriotic Americans in this nation. Kyoto would have gone down in flames in the United States Senate, and China is no fan of international agreements requiring it think about its own massive pollution during this phase of intensive industrialization. At the same time, The White House argued that they would take on the issue effectively but many people question their sincerity.

Representing all of us in the United States and treating the entire world like they exist for our pleasure the administration looked, once again, like the idiot bully making fun of all the other kids on the playground. It doesn't take long before no one plays with the bully. This is the backdrop for the nations who worked in Bali. Enjoying humid weather in a tropical forest which, given current international industrial regimes, may not be there by the time our youngest children are old enough to read.

They discussed cap and trade regimes in the belief the market will provide the greatest regulatory fulfillment of need. However, some of us are not thrilled with the possibilities of this due to market failures.

If it is cheaper to dump effluent into the river, and a corporation can get away with it, the waste is going into the river. Stockholders want profit and multi-national executives make a fair chunk of change making sure stockholders are happy. It is just too bad if Togo is lost. Maybe the people can be transported to Nauru.

It is difficult to imagine and then create new, top heavy international regimes. People here in the States are not likely to look kindly on executive orders coming from Ban Ki Moon. International authority doesn't stand a chance in Iowa. No U.N. leader, no matter what their motivations, will revel in heartland voters' sympathy anytime soon.

And that leads us back with the Chinese. Those wily capitalist pigs, as they used to call us, clawing up the back of the American standard bearer because this nation has the mentality to avoid production on our own soil due to environmental and human rights legislation which protects workers, land, and air while strapping the middle class with a growing dependency on the cheap trash manufactured overseas or south of the border.

As soon as the Chinese discover the payoff from the creation of a middle class, they will be making yen hands over fists and won't be so worried about the measly three hundred odd million Americans buying their wares. So what if they can't see the sky and will never drink the water? They bottle it now and most people are content to stay inside playing Wii. Never underestimate the Chinese sense of purpose and the drive for wealth that has made our nation what it is. If Canada can't meet its proposed targets and Russia doesn't care, what will be made of poor Kyoto, the last piece of garbage for the trash heap of international relations history?

W promised to protect the country though. Once he told us to buy…buy stuff, lots of it, right now because terrorists want to deny our Constitutional right to get low-priced goods from the international market. Someone needs to research whether, in his speech after this nation was attacked by a group of Neanderthal hit men looking to Allah for praise in heaven in the form of whiskey and wild women, he mentioned buy American. It seems doubtful. I never heard it. Just buy. Buy lots. It is true. It works…for a while.

However, when the debts are tallied and the votes are in, our environmental health is in a more precarious state than seven years ago. This leaves a lot of folks pondering what exactly this President has done to earn our trust and respect. Simply being voted into office does not give anyone, let alone his or her subordinates, lackeys, and spin doctors, the right to run rampant over our environmental regulations. Be that as it may, the last stand of the commander in chief could have been avoided and was completely unnecessary if he had made different choices along the way. If he had listened.

Bush was uninterested in things like the Bali Conference which required working with some form of opposition. The lesson to learn here is the tragedy of cowboy diplomacy and take-no-prisoners policies. This type of blind leadership is bad for the country. We also need to realize that the inability and unwillingness to listen to those who think differently leaves the country worse off than it should be.

Through Bush's tenure, he showed disdain for anyone disagreeing with him or his fanatic cronies, who he hired to conduct our business. He gave a personal commitment to taking global warming seriously and then blew off concerted efforts of dedicated individuals working to get something, anything, done at Bali.

Participants at Bali, like many of our own citizens, became determined to simply wait him out. It will not be surprising if George W. Bush goes down as the greatest fool of the twenty-first century. Historians may say they believe he was blind, deaf, and dumb, without a care in the world for anyone but his own party faithful.

The shame of the Bali conference, as with so many aspects of international diplomacy under Bush, is that the United States should have taken a prominent role. The President could have done so much more with some small gestures of good will and if he just paid a little bit of attention. Instead he took the cowboy stand. At least he has shown us what not to do in the future.

Ten Solutions

I went to the woods because I wished to live deliberately, to front only the essential facts of life, and see if I could not learn what it had to teach, and not, when I came to die, discover that I had not lived.[4]

~Henry David Thoreau, 1854

American energy and resourcefulness offer solutions to most of the challenges driving the public discourse about nature. We need to discuss priorities if we are to generate positive notions about society and the environment. So often, connections to the past blur our vision. There is so much to do and such a list of things that can be done if business, individuals, and government participate fully in investing for environmental health. Corporate America needs to act. Business leaders need to think about how their dealings guide the rest of the people while pursuing their own goals and moving ahead. They also need to be involved in the social and economic transformations necessary for a cleaner environment and healthier communities.

It has already been noted: people around the world look to the United States for guidance, information, knowledge, and hope. Therefore, we can and should be out front in the conversion to renewable resources and cleaner business practices. There is no need to fear the rest of the world. With the rise in industrial capacity in both China and India, as well as much of the rest of the world, competition for natural resources is rising to alarming levels. Our current trends of consumption are in opposition to the continued reliance on fossil fuels.

The world of tomorrow is found in renewable energy and we can lead the way.

Solar energy needs more research, but so do coal and natural gas. The search for resources can be destructive and environmental impacts are often severe. We need to wake up and realize there is no drilling out of this spectacular hole we find ourselves trapped in. If those looking to open ANWR get their way, they will not be crafting solutions to coming problems, but they will only be prolonging the inevitable. New methods of energy production and preservation are the wave of the future. A cornucopia of resolutions is available to those willing to act by cleaning up the land. No single prescription will bring us out of the darkness but we have to combine all technologies and rely on all of our knowledge.

The following list is short and not meant to be comprehensive. It is only an overview of some of the biggest areas of concern and how we may be able to deal with them. It also provides some of the easiest things we can all do in our everyday lives to limit our emissions and reduce our collective footprint.

1. Coal:

Coal provides over fifty per cent of the energy used in our country. Supporting this filthy type of power has gained national attention through the focus on "clean coal" technology. This involves the use of scrubbers to reduce the amount of carbon escaping from coal fired power plants, using "cleaner coal", or capturing carbon in the ground. Billions of dollars have been invested by the Bush administration into clean coal technology. Coal has a terrible carbon footprint and those in the industry have proven to be reticent to ramp up the cleaner technology because they are prohibitively expensive.

One way massive coal corporations have focused on reducing expenses and making things safer is to conduct mountaintop mining. In the process, the tops of mountains are simply removed to get at the coal seams much more quickly. Aside from the horrid aesthetic consequences, mountaintop mining strips the land of its natural cover, reduces the richness of the soil, exposes areas to excessive runoff, and endangers lives.

The government needs to ban mountaintop mining immediately and demand coal and utility companies use the cleanest technologies for all coal fired power plants. They also need to require safety measures for miners. We are not getting away from coal. So we need to proceed with great caution, perhaps close down older facilities, and press for new methods of developing our lands and using our resources.

2. Oil:

Oil's unfavorable view in the United States will continue to dominate headlines and create strife while our reliance upon it continues unabated. The Bush administration took every step possible to increase domestic production but this has done nothing to assuage the needs to send money to tyrannical oil producing nations and this is unlikely to change without some serious actions taken to heal our addiction. Every possible area could be opened to exploration and exploitation tomorrow and it will not dent international markets or the need for oil from foreign sources on U.S. soil.

Our reliance on oil is not going away within anyone's lifetime. Our lifestyle is too intertwined with the stuff. Production, consumption, and transportation rely on black crude. Everything in today's world uses oil somewhere along the line. The concern generated by giant corporate oil producers show they wish to continue controlling the wealth of nations. We all just need to figure out how to reduce the influence of oil.

3. The Automobile Industry:

The American automobile industry is experiencing difficulties due to past labor relations but executives still gather enormous paychecks and people do not want to buy their cars because of a perception of shoddy performance and ignorance of long term desires. The SUV is supported due to safety and size and it isn't going away. It is hard to fit a soccer team in a small car. It is impossible to get off-road or through mountain snow without four wheel drive and trucks still hold the top spot of American auto sales. But we are relying on vehicles which use more fuel than is prudent given our current situation, and American car makers are suffering because of a change in public attitude.

Despite facts showing public adoration of the large vehicle, folks are starting to demand greater fuel efficiency and reliability in their cars and trucks. Detroit can ride this wave back to the top of the sound fiscal mountain if they focus technology into producing better cars people will want and ramp up the pace of advances so they leave any increase in café standards in the dust. People will then see the need and the benefits of buying American again.

4. Railroads:

Amtrak has fought bankruptcy for years and the government is constantly faced with bailing out the terminally ill public corporation. However, railroads present unique opportunities for transportation which continues to grow in importance as populations rise and traffic congestion becomes more unbearable. Numerous cities have moved to take advantage of high speed commuter rail to reduce congestion and give alternatives to city dwellers. The problem is always cost and the irritability of tax payers to one more grand scheme they see as robbing them of their earnings.

5. Alternative Transportation:

Biking is an easy way to reduce your carbon footprint and it is obvious why. Along with a greater emphasis on biking, a new era can be ushered in for the biking industry. They are certainly cheaper than cars and they keep people healthy, reduce traffic, get people outdoors, and generally are a good way to capture the modern imagination.

We need to develop good bike lanes and safety measures aimed to make it more enticing to hop on a bike to get to and from work and around town to make this really take off. Many cities around the country are focusing on making biking a more attractive option.

6. Composting:

Composting keeps food litter and biodegradable material out of public landfills. It generates rich fertilizer and can be used to foster efforts to grow food and flowers at home, thus bringing people closer with nature. Many of us do not have the time or space to be involved in composting but many do and they are doing a wonderful thing. Every little bit helps.

7. Green Building:

Environmental optimism is nowhere more promising than in construction. Green buildings use timber collected from certified forests, recycled material when possible, solar panels, wind turbines, rooftop gardens, reclaimed water, and locally natural landscaping. In green building, there is a focus on better insulation which reduces the need for excessive heating and cooling.

It is really just smart for both business and consumers. A more insulated building will not cost so much to heat. Solar panels and wind turbines can eliminate electrical bills and, in some places, they can even generate refunds if they are hooked into the grid and they provide power back into the system. Additionally, the nation has seen major power outages in recent years resulting from the dependency on centralized power. Localized electrical solutions such as solar and wind reduce drains on the grid.

8. Solar Power:

Solar holds a lot of promise. It reduces the necessity to rely upon coal fired and nuclear plants. Solar needs research to be more cost effective and efficient and the federal government should support research into solar alternatives and subsidize power companies and homeowners making investments in solar. Yes, these are payments but there are times when industry needs to receive incentives from the federal government to get started and to provide the needed investment opportunities which can lead to advancements in technology.

There are those who would balk at providing any sort of break to businesses working on issues of solar power but their voices are often silent in the case of current subsidies for existing industries like oil, gas, coal, and nuclear. We need a smarter, more comprehensive energy policy.

9. Wind Turbines:

Massive wind farms already grace the landscape in the U.S. and a growing percentage of the country's electricity comes from wind energy. Conflicts arise even from wind energy because of a danger to birds and for aesthetic reasons, keeping turbines away from offshore areas.

But the energy is clean, renewable, and it creates good paying jobs in the energy sector which, at least for a while, will not be available for outsourcing. I'm sure some type of control can be located overseas but maintenance and upkeep will always be local. Wind power provides such wonderful opportunities, we need to keep it at the forefront of our debates.

10. Lighting:

Lights are all the rage these days. An imperative has been set out due to the conversation over carbon emissions and global warming to people to change their light bulbs and to use more efficient lighting. This reduces the impact on power plants and increases efficiency. Changing lights is something everyone can do without the investments necessary to put solar or wind powered elements into existing structures.

So many things are being done and will continue to be done to counteract environmental impacts which arise from an industrial society conducting business in the same fashion for over 100 years. Americans need to show the way to industrializing nations like China and India and demonstrate to these cultures how action can be taken without negatively affecting the social order or economic success.

The real tension between protecting our environment and growing our economy is from our old conceptions about what is possible and how we conceive the changes needed to form a new world. We can still conduct business which takes the environment into consideration. Public support for environmental initiatives is strong. It is one more area, however, that we need to get beyond the old battles and move on.

The More Things Change

When the Constitution was adopted, at the end of the eighteenth century, no human wisdom could foretell the sweeping changes, alike in industrial and political conditions, which were to take place by the beginning of the twentieth century.[5]

~Theodore Roosevelt, 1901

Environmental issues can bring us together. Many of us support environmental industries. We need to think about how we conduct business, however, because past short sightedness reduced old growth forests, polluted waterways, and harmed public health. Tree huggers and tree cutters have begun to sit down together to renew forest health but their partnership is tenuous at this point. However, it is unlikely we will make any progress in an war waged for wealth and influence.

Environmental politics encompasses the complexity of our nation. It involves relationships between: economics, biology, forestry, journalism, business, history, ecology, development, interest groups, negotiation, finance, philosophy, and, of course, political realities. It is an area rich in the social and natural sciences. It affects private land-owners, public spaces, business, social networks, and it is couched in idealism. Nature influences our thoughts of what it is to be human and how we think as Americans. It is central to who we are.

There are those who claim we can do no wrong and that, on a geologic scale, whatever we do will be a drop in the bucket and nature will recover. Nature will heal herself over time. We need to consider, though, what we want to protect when we defend our environment. What will it look like while we are living in it?

For a long time, nature was seen as a potent adversary, yet our ancestors thrived with their knowledge of it as well. Environmental preservation is at the heart of our politics. As much as national pride swells from an unstoppable USA basketball team, or an underdog USA hockey team, or the soldiers' actions in far away lands, the roots of our stability and growth can be uncovered within the contours of our land.

Chapter Eleven: Conclusion

Creativity and Possibility

Afoot and lighthearted, I take to the open road,
Healthy, free, the world before me,
The long brown path before me, leading wherever I choose.
Henceforth, I ask not good fortune—I myself am good fortune;
Henceforth I whimper no more, postpone no more, need nothing,
Strong and content, I travel the open road.[1]

~Walt Whitman, 1900

What an appealing vision of freedom Walt had so many years ago. "Song of the Open Road" should be considered essential reading to anyone pondering such lofty subjects as liberty and the meaning of America. He reminds us the road is hard and it will toughen those who travel upon it but it is open to all who wish to experience its wonders and its rewards are many. It is a splendid allegory for our country.

The parameters exist in the structure of the republic to solve problems collectively. We will always believe the future outshines the past and tomorrow we will be stronger and wiser than we are today. As a nation, we can meet any challenge, advance with opportunity, and strive for heights surpassing our dreams. All it takes is a little faith, perseverance, a lot of effort, and a bit more conversation.

Striving together, we can get beyond the petty and simple arguments offered in place of true deliberation. To do this, we must hold elected officials and the media accountable. Nobody has time to read everything necessary to fully grasp the intricate workings of government. It is always easy to take cheap shots at politicians. We need to remember, though, in a republic, elected officials are merely a reflection of ourselves.

It is astonishing anyone becomes a civil servant at all. Giving your life up to the unscrupulous scrutiny of press and opposition renders many able and patriotic individuals unwilling to serve the public.

Politics can be decent or perverse. The results are up to us. To think we have no control over our destiny is to suppose the system doesn't matter at all—the United States of America is just a meaningless, monolithic monster motivated by greed and run by half wit brutes favoring sex slaves and feeding on raw meat. And then, all the ideals would be futile.

Captivating as such a story is, it fails to account for the progress in human rights, science, environmental knowledge, and free thought which has been generated in this nation. Our country is great because of a proud and revered history. We should never forget this.

If you are angry, get active and do something. If there are things bothering you, help get things changed. Stand up, speak your mind, get off the couch and make some noise. When they ignore you, rock the boat a bit more, vote. Or don't. It is completely up to you but don't be shocked at the results if you don't take part in some form. The essence of freedom is that it is your choice.

Read beyond the mainstream. Read conservative, liberal, and independent thinkers. Without holding on to some overwhelming connection to one ideology, understand that other views may benefit your own. It is important to take a stand but it takes mental courage to listen and learn.

This generation must assess what it is to be American. What does it mean to "support the general welfare?" What does it mean for a parent to raise children with two or three jobs and no health care? What does it mean to educate children? How can the country affirm the position as defender of liberty when the ultimate acts of society point towards working conditions fostering fear and repression? $7.00 per hour is an ugly wage for an adult. These are not foolish, pie in the sky inquiries with no answers but essential for ensuring a strong and stable republic and we should not fear to ask them.

So much is possible if we take some chances and rely on creativity. If we protect nature, use a little less, respect a little more, demand transparency in government, and practice a smarter economics we may be surprised at the results.

We can reduce the size of government by conducting social enterprises more intelligently, not by running government as if it is a business because it is not.

We must insist on accountability and responsibility. Without this we just trade governmental totalitarianism for corporate oppression. Corporate leaders need to realize that they make their profits from working Americans and the more stability there is in society, the safer their earnings. Industry leaders must take the important actions required of their lofty positions and they should lead the way with integrity and honor. In America, all things are possible.

America Can Still Lead the World
Be not quick to anger, for anger lodges in the bosom of fools.[2]

~Ecclesiastes, 7:9

I've tried with this book to place current events and political dialogue within a historical framework. I did this to show that the past is important, politics can be noble, and we are lucky to live in a magnificent nation. We all could work to heighten our awareness in how we govern ourselves.

I don't know if it is truly possible to see the world through clear lenses—unfiltered by bias and pre-conceptions. Ideological affiliation is often apparent when people discuss politics but it is never so simple.

Personally, I want smaller government but one which takes account of modern reality. I look for personal responsibility but expect corporate and civic accountability as well. I desire liberty above all but true liberty of the will not just economic license. I would like to see a strong but diplomatic foreign policy. Finally, I trust that we can learn how to choose wisely when considering future options but the only way we will is to open our discussions into areas where we are, at times, uncomfortable. We have to talk to those with whom we disagree.

We have to regain ownership of our institutions and elevate pride of citizenship. To do this, we need to share knowledge with each other, discuss how we got here, and choose where we want to go. What sort of society do we wish to construct for the future? We have to be careful when choosing leadership because governing on unadulterated ideology is rarely constructive.

Each side pledges to solve all problems with their plans. However, all promised utopias wither on the vine of human experience. They are quickly perverted and promises of a conflict-free world engineer a track to tyranny. In order to avoid tyranny, every generation must answer the question posed by Alexander Hamilton quoted in the introduction...is good government possible?

If the system is broken, let's alter it. It is made to withstand all but the most venal of threats. To fix anything, it is vital that we hear each other. Through opening our minds to divergent thinking, concerns are uncovered allowing us to craft a strong, safe, and fair nation for tomorrow. Never will it be said of America that free debate brought it down.

It is easy to simplify political arguments, demonize the opposition, and build authoritarian systems. Intricacy lies in considering our true history and thinking of the struggles which won the freedoms we enjoy today. Democracy is not painless and the work never ends.

Freedom and Justice

I took right hold of the cause. I could do but little; but what I could, I did with a joyful heart.[3]

~Frederick Douglass, 1845

Frederick Douglass is an American hero. His sentiments provide a glimpse into the anti-slavery movement in New England. As a former slave, he assumed his role would be small...it is easy to perceive how, at first, he was convinced he could not "fight city hall." Still, he embraced the struggle for freedom and he was overjoyed being involved. Alas, he would become one of our greatest thinkers, activists, and writers. How uniquely American! We can learn from Douglass. He had the option to withdraw from society, move on with life, and forge an existence on his own but he dreamed of a new day where justice prevailed and so he worked, studied, and altered destiny. How cool is that?

Authority should be challenged. The preservation of liberty and the pursuit of justice demand it. If they are in the right, they have nothing to fear. Some argue it is best to shade our eyes and trust the judgment of the powerful. I say our ancestors would never have dared revolution without a healthy disrespect for authority. Justice is elusive and it must be pursued. Liberty takes many forms and we must be vigilant so that we do not confuse the essence of its teachings. Keep in mind, I am not arguing we should exhibit contempt for authority but we need to strive for fairness while protecting individual free will.

This entire book is my humble effort to support our nation and our ideals by elevating our discussions. But sometimes we are required by what we hold true to stand against the status quo and take on the elites. In doing so non-violently, thoughtfully, passionately, vigorously, and with forethought, we are defended by the very framework of government designed by the Constitution and embodied in the Declaration of Independence. I may be wrong but it is my right and duty to express what I believe to be harmful to society, a hindrance to freedom, or a barrier to justice. And I am bound to hear those who would condemn me.

So much of the way we conduct politics leads to overlooking positive alternatives, heightened bitterness, the loss of civility, increased partisan rancor, corruption, and the loss of protection for the most valued American treasures. The free market is key but so are free speech, free expression, and free thought. Folks yearn to be free from fear, despair, poverty, starvation, racism, and homelessness. We also need the freedom to work, save, invest, start businesses, and control our earnings. And we want to hire competent, conscientious, hard working, and honest representatives.

It must be hard to turn down a quick ski junket including the finest accommodations and a private plane to attend a conference discussing why Yellowstone needs to be privatized and bulldozed for gated ranchettes. Luckily, the framers of the Constitution knew about things such as human frailty and the seduction of material wealth and the

124

tyranny arising out of unbridled supremacy of any faction. They were able to create a structure of government which defended against human weakness in the face of power. Still, it is hard to protect the republic if citizens don't believe we have the right or the ability to do so.

Life in America is a wondrous gift. It is amazing, intriguing, and it grows through peace and tragedy. The collectively shared life is acted out on the political stage. We have been bequeathed a great endowment from those who tread the waters before us. All they asked is that we keep our spirit alive with our thoughts and that we keep vigilant.

The Shining City on a Hill[4]

You are the light of the world. A city set on a hill cannot be hid.[5]
~Jesus of Nazareth: Mathew, 5:14

What ever happened to the Greek city states like Athens, the world's first known foray into democracy? How did Rome fall after over one thousand years? Greece lost their way to more powerful foes and Rome experienced the death of empire...the republic did not fair well or last long. The Weimar Republic, the erstwhile democracy preceding Adolph Hitler in Germany was erased when the little nazi gained ultimate muscle as chancellor. Democracies often fail. They are inefficient and slow to act, people don't blindly follow rulers in democracies, and if bread is scarce liberty appears to be just an odd theory instead of being the cornerstone strengthening the rest of society.

James Madison crafted one of the most powerful forces in history...The Constitution. It guides us and it is a symbol of hope for millions around the globe who believe that here they can follow their dreams and realize their aspirations. Worldwide, people are inspired by freedom and the ability to transcend class boundaries with hard work and dedication. Freedom is the greatest gift we have. Let's not lose it.

America is alive and well but we need to re-capture the spirit which makes our country the hope of humanity. Petty political squabbles corrupt the system but there is something deeper which strengthens us. Laughter in spite of adversity enlivens our souls. We are generous and giving, willing to send aid to other nations, even so-called enemies, at a moments notice. It is amazing, really, the openness we have as a society.

Boxes of grain opened by North Koreans captures their imagination regarding our country. Aid to Banda Ache engendered encouraging feelings for the U.S. in the minds of millions of Indonesians. Our kindness knows few bounds. We want to help others achieve independence and freedom while keeping safe and enjoying our own economic success. These are good, strong qualities.

It is hard to figure out what has happened to our optimism. Neither liberals nor conservatives stole away in the night with the American dream. It would be frighteningly easy to blame the media and the pundits for seeking negativity and bad news around every corner as if they were laughing their way to the bank on the misery of the masses but we are the ones who support their businesses. We can censure the courts, accuse the lawyers and the millionaires, balk at scandal and strife emanating from morally bankrupt Hollywood, or tax the oily greedheads raping the land. None of this will restore our fundamental confidence in our nation.

We must learn that the American dream is not really dead; all of the icons have simply ignored it for so long it has soured and left a bad taste in the mouths of generations. It needs to be re-captured, renewed, and revitalized. The world will forever look to the United States as long as our inner compass guides the way towards a grand and just future.

Notes and Bibliography

Introduction

1. Hamilton, Alexander. 1788. Federalist #1. In, *James Madison, Alexander Hamilton, and John Jay, The Federalist Papers.* Edited by Issac Kramnick. Penguin Books. New York. 1987. This collection of essays first appeared in 1787 and they were published collectively in 1788. The Federalist Papers materialized in the New York *Independent Journal* on October 27, 1787. They are a group of essays defending the Constitution and aimed to convince the public of the importance and efficacy of the new government in the hopes the public would support the ratification of the Constitution.
2. President Bush warned the rest of the world to watch out when he spoke in front of both houses of Congress and the American people, pitting our interests against any who would question our divine right to conduct international relations however we see fit. The exact quote during this particular speech, given on September 20, 2001 is: "every nation, in every region, now has a decision to make. Either you are with us, or you are with the terrorists." This quote was accessed on the web 4-3-2008 at the White House website:
    www.whitehouse.gov/news/releases/2001/09/20010920-8.html

Chapter One

1. The Preamble to the U.S. Constitution. In, *We the People: An Introduction to American Politics, Fourth Edition.* Benjamin Gindsberg, Theodore J. Lowi, and Margaret Weir. Norton, New York. 2003.
2. The Declaration of Independence. In, *We the People: An Introduction to American Politics, Fourth Edition.* Benjamin Gindsberg, Theodore J. Lowi, and Margaret Weir. Norton, New York. 2003.

3. De Tocqueville, Alexis. 1835. *Democracy in America.* In, *Democracy in America: The Conplete and Unabridged Volumes I and II,* Translated by Henry Reeve. Introduction by Joseph Epstein. Bantam, New York. 2000. De Tocqueville traveled the U.S. over nine months between 1831 and 1832. He wrote what became on of the most influential and comprehensive treatises concerning America's democracy, customs, laws, and driving forces, publishing it in 1835.

4. Executive Office of the President of the United States. Accessed online 3-24-2008: www.gpoaccess.gov/usbudget/

5. Bureau of Labor. Accessed online 3-24-2008: www.bls.gov/oco/cg/cgs041.htm

6. Barbaro, Michael. 2008. March 3. International Herald Tribune. Accessed online 3-24-2008: www.iht.com/articles/2008/03/03/technology/walmart.php

7. Thoreau, Henry David. 1849. *Civil Disobedience.* Signet, New York. 1980. Thoreau places this in quotation marks and it is attributed all over the web to Thomas Paine and, at times, to Thomas Jefferson. I did not find a single mention of where either one said or wrote it. The place I know this quote from is Thoreau.

8. Madison, James. 1788. Federalist #51. In, *James Madison, Alexander Hamilton, and John Jay, The Federalist Papers.* Edited by Isaac Kramnick. Penguin Books, New York. 1987.

9. Madison, James. Federalist #51. In, *James Madison, Alexander Hamilton, and John Jay, The Federalist Papers.* Edited by Isaac Kramnick. Penguin Books, New York. 1987.

Chapter Two

1. Thompson, Hunter. 2003. *The Great Shark Hunt.* Simon and Schuster. New York. (First Published in The Boston Globe, Feb 23, 1969)

2. "The nanny state" is a popular derogatory term used to demean the United States federal government and to compare it with

socialist doctrine. It is a common attack on active government in modern times. Representative Ron Paul used the term derisively in repeated stump speeches during his run for the White House in 2007 and 2008.

3. Limbaugh, Rush. 1992. *The Way Things Ought to Be.* Pocket Books, a division of Symon and Schuster, New York.
4. Limbaugh, Rush. 1992. *The Way Things Ought to Be.* Pocket Books, a division of Symon and Schuster, New York.
5. Limbaugh, Rush. 1992. *The Way Things Ought to Be.* Pocket Books, a division of Symon and Schuster, New York.
6. Limbaugh, Rush. 1992. *The Way Things Ought to Be.* Pocket Books, a division of Symon and Schuster, New York.
7. Limbaugh, Rush. 1992. *The Way Things Ought to Be.* Pocket Books, a division of Symon and Schuster, New York.
8. Goldwater, Barry. 1960. *The Conscience of a Conservative.* Princeton University Press, Princeton. 2007. Originally published in 1960 by Victor Publishing Inc.
9. Henry, Patrick. 1788. In: *The Anti-Federalist Papers and the Constitutional Debates.* Edited by Ralph Ketcham. New American Library, New York. 1986.
10. First Amendment to the Constitution. In, *We the People: An Introduction to American Politics, Fourth Edition.* Benjamin Gindsberg, Theodore J. Lowi, and Margaret Weir. Norton, New York. 2003.
11. Henry, Patrick. 1788. In: *The Anti-Federalist Papers and the Constitutional Debates.* Edited by Ralph Ketcham. New American Library, New York. 1986.
12. Brainy Quote.com. Accessed on 4-3-2008: www.brainyquote.com/quotes/authors/r/ronald_reagan.html
13. Jefferson, Thomas. 1826. In, *The Life and Selected Writings of Thomas Jefferson.* Edited by Adrienne Koch and William Paden. Modern Library, New York. 2004.

Chapter Three
1. Goldwater, Barry. 1960. *The Conscience of a Conservative.* Princeton University Press, Princeton. 2007. Originally published in 1960 by Victor Publishing Inc.
2. Hamilton, Alexander. 1788. Federalist #1. In, *James Madison, Alexander Hamilton, and John Jay, The Federalist Papers.* Edited by Isaac Kramnick. Penguin Books, New York. 1987.
3. Roosevelt, Franklin D. 1933. First Inaugural Address. In: *Our Nation's Archive: The History of the United States in Documents.* Edited by Erik Bruun and Jay Crosby. Black Dog and Leventhal, New York. 1999.
4. Holy Bible. Revised Standard Version.
5. De Tocqueville, Alexis. 1835. *Democracy in America.* In, *Democracy in America: The Conplete and Unabridged Volumes I and II,* Translated by Henry Reeve. Introduction by Joseph Epstein. Bantam, New York. 2000.
6. The National Park Service (NPS). All information relating to the NPS is available on its website. Accessed 3-10-2008: www.nps.gov.
7. According to the New Dictionary on Cultural Literacy, the full statement—"power tends to corrupt, absolute power corrupts absolutely," is attributed to Lord Acton, and English historian who lived in the late 1800s and into the 1900s. Accessed on 3-10-2008: www.bartleby.com/59/13/powertendsto.html.
8. Clinton, William J. 1996. Radio Address. January 27. Accessed on the web 4-3-08 on CNN: www.cnn.com/US/9601/budget/01-27/clinton_radio/

Chapter Four
1. Madison, James. 1788. Federalist #10. In, *James Madison, Alexander Hamilton, and John Jay, The Federalist Papers.* Edited by Isaac Kramnick. Penguin Books, New York. 1987.
2. Hunter, Kathleen. 2005. Interview with Homeland Security Chief Joe Moore. January 25. Accessed online 3-24-2008:

www.stateline.org/live/ViewPage.action?siteNodeId=136&lang uageId=1&contentId=15938

3. Salt Lake Tribune. 2006. January 6. Accessed online 3-24-2008: cms.firehouse.com/web/online/Terrorism-and-Front-Lines/Utah-May-Take-Hit-In-Safety-Funding/1$46735

4. Sophocles, *Oedipus the King.*

5. Aeschylus, *Agamemnon*

6. Holy Bible. Revised Standard Version.

7. Thoreau, Henry David. 1854. *Walden, or Life in the Woods.* Signet, New York. 1980.

8. About.com. Accessed 3-24-2008: uspolitics.about.com/od/polls/l/bl_historical_approval.htm

9. Dickens, Charles. 1843. *A Christmas Carol.* In Charles Dickens: Complete and Unabridged. Barnes and Noble, New York. 2006.

10. Thoreau, Henry David. 1849. *Civil Disobedience.* Signet, New York. 1980.

Chapter Five

1. Niemoller, Pastor Martin. 1946. The origin of the quote seems to be a bit of a mystery, even to the pastor himself. There are numerous versions of this quote available on the web and it is difficult to distinguish which is the most accurate. Here the version quoted is from a plaque at the New England Holocaust Museum. Accessed online 3-31-2008: www.nehm.org/contents/niemoller.html.

2. King Jr., Dr. Martin Luther. 1968. *Remaining Awake Through a Great Revolution.* In, *A Testament of Hope: The Essential Writings of Martin Luther King Jr.* Edited by James M. Washington. Harper and Row, San Francisco. 1986.

3. Roosevelt, Franklin D. 1933. Statement on the National Industrial Recovery Act. June 16. Accessed online at FDR Presidential Library: www.fdrlibrary.marist.edu/odnirast.html.

4. Declaration of Independence. In, *We the People: An Introduction to American Politics, Fourth Edition.* Benjamin

Gindsberg, Theodore J. Lowi, and Margaret Weir. Norton, New York. 2003.

Chapter Six: Fiscal Responsibility

1. Thoreau, Henry David. 1854. *Walden, or Life in the Woods.* Signet, New York. 1980.
2. Greenspan, Alan. 2007. *The Age of Turbulence: Adventures in a New World.* Penguin, New York.
3. The transcript of this interchange is available at MSNBC. Accessed on 4-3-2008: www.msnbc.msn.com/id/5892840/
4. Gingrich, Newt, Dick Armey, and the House Republicans. 1994. *Contract with America: The Bold Plan by Rep. Newt Gingrich, Rep. Dick Armey, and the House Republicans to Change the Nation.* Times Books, New York.
5. Greenspan, Alan. 2007. *The Age of Turbulence: Adventures in a New World.* Penguin, New York.
6. Populist Party Platform, 1892. In, *Our Nation's Archive: The History of the United States in Documents.* Edited by Erik Bruun and Jay Crosby. Black Dog and Levinthal Publishers, Inc. New York. 1999.
7. Roosevelt, Theodore. 1901. His first inaugural address. In, *Our Nation's Archive: The History of the United States in Documents.* Edited by Erik Bruun and Jay Crosby. Black Dog and Levinthal, New York. 1999.

Chapter Seven: Foreign Policy

1. Eisenhower, Dwight D. Farewell Address to the Nation. 1961. In, *Our Nation's Archive: The History of the United States in Documents.* Edited by Erik Bruun and Jay Crosby. Black Dog and Levinthal, New York. 1999.
2. The American Heritage Dictionary, Fourth Edition. 2001. Dell Publishing, New York.

3. Jay, John. 1788. Federalist #5. In, *James Madison, Alexander Hamilton, and John Jay, The Federalist Papers.* Edited by Issac Kramnick. Penguin Books, New York. 1987.
4. John McCain used waving the white flag repeatedly to show how Democrats wished to surrender in Iraq and subsequently the "War on Terror." His warning was clear—anyone who disagrees with him or his party wants America to lose.
5. Holy Bible. Revised Standard Version.
6. Holy Bible. Revised Standard Version.
7. Lincoln, Abraham. 1863. Address at Gettysburg, Pennsylvania, November 19. In, *Abraham Lincoln: Speeches and Writings 1859-1865.* Literary Classics, New York. 1989.
8. Declaration of Independence. In, *We the People: An Introduction to American Politics, Fourth Edition.* Benjamin Gindsberg, Theodore J. Lowi, and Margaret Weir. Norton, New York. 2003.

Chapter Eight: Morality

1. Lincoln, Abraham. 1859. Address to the Wisconsin State Agricultural Society, Milwaukee, Wisconsin, September 30. In *Abraham Lincoln: Speeches and Writings 1859-1865.* Literary Classics, New York. 1989.
2. Holy Bible. Revised Standard Version.
3. Fourth Amendment to the U.S. Constitution. In, *We the People: An Introduction to American Politics, Fourth Edition.* Benjamin Gindsberg, Theodore J. Lowi, and Margaret Weir. Norton, New York. 2003.
4. Jay, John. 1788. Federalist #2. In, *James Madison, Alexander Hamilton, and John Jay, The Federalist Papers.* Edited by Isaac Kramnick. Penguin Books, New York. 1987.
5. The United States Constitution. In, *We the People: An Introduction to American Politics, Fourth Edition.* Benjamin Gindsberg, Theodore J. Lowi, and Margaret Weir. Norton, New York. 2003.

Chapter Nine: Religion

1. Eisenhower, Dwight D. Farewell Address to the Nation. 1961. Miller Center for Public Affairs, The University of Virginia. Accessed online 4-3-2008: millercenter.org/scripps/archive/speeches/detail/3361
2. Holy Bible. Revised Standard Version.
3. Infoplease. Accessed 3-20-2008: www.infoplease.com/ipa/A0781450.html
4. Infoplease. Accessed 3-20-2008: www.infoplease.com/ipa/A0781450.html
5. Holy Bible. Revised Standard Version.
6. First Amendment to the U.S. Constitution. In, *We the People: An Introduction to American Politics, Fourth Edition.* Benjamin Gindsberg, Theodore J. Lowi, and Margaret Weir. Norton, New York. 2003.
7. U.S. Census. Accessed online 4-3-2008: www.census.gov/

Chapter Ten: The Environment

1. Roosevelt, Theodore. 1907. Seventh Annual Message to Congress, December 3. PBS: Accessed online 4-3-2008: http://www.pbs.org/weta/thewest/resources/archives/eight/trcon serv.htm.
2. Muir, John. In, *The Wilderness World of John Muir: A Selection From His Collected Work.* Edited by Edwin Way Teale. 2001. Houghtan Mifflin, New York. There is no date on this quotation as it is a random writing, according to Teale.
3. Bush, George W. 2007. Remarks at the U.S. Department of State. September 27. Accessed online 4-3-2008, www.state.gov/g/oes/rls/rm/2007/92938.htm
4. Thoreau, Henry David. 1854. *Walden, or Life in the Woods.* Signet, New York. 1980.
5. Roosevelt, Theodore. 1901. Annual Message to Congress. December 3. In, *Our Nation's Archive: The History of the United States in Documents.* Edited by Erik Bruun and Jay Crosby. Black Dog and Levinthal, New York. 1999.

Chapter Eleven: Conclusion

1. Whitman, Walt. 1900. *Leaves of Grass*. Bartleby.com. Accessed online 4-3-2008: www.bartleby.com/142/82.html.
2. Holy Bible. Revised Standard Version.
3. Douglass, Frederick. 1845. *Narrative of the Life of Frederick Douglass: An American Slave.* Introduction by Milliam Mackey Jr. Barnes and Noble, New York. 2002.
4. Ronald Reagan used this in many speeches over his long political career to describe our country. In his farewell address, he attributed the speech to John Winthrop, a pilgrim who became the governor of the Massachusetts Bay Colony. It describes a society of freedom which provides guidance to others. Its origins can be found in scripture. Reagan Foundation Website. Accessed 4-3-2008:
www.reaganfoundation.org/reagan/speeches/farewell.asp
5. Holy Bible. Revised Standard Version.

About the Author

James Douglas Buthman was born and raised outside Chicago, Illinois. After many years in the private sector, he is currently living as a writer and a student of the United States at the base of the San Francisco Peaks in Flagstaff, Arizona with his girlfriend, Jean, and their three dogs, Marley, Spike, and Zoe. An American citizen, he has traveled the country extensively by plane, train, car, by foot, and on a bicycle. He received his Bachelor's degree in political science from Colorado State University in 1993 and his Master's degree in political science from Northern Arizona University in 2006. He edits the online journal Politics and Nature, located at www.politicsandnature.com.

Printed in the United States
112910LV00001B/10-183/P

9 781601 454966